7/2/92

Dear Al -
 Here are some new and different thoughts to dwell upon in the attics. Hope it all comes together soon!
 Love
 Mom

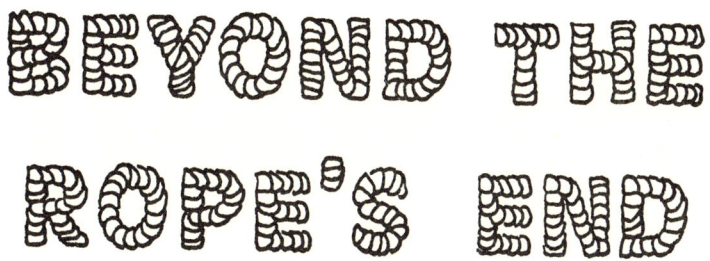

BEYOND THE ROPE'S END

ROBERT E. ROSS
Certified Psychologist

A PERSONAL POWER POTENTIAL BOOK

Copyright 1982 by Personal Power Potential

All rights reserved. No part of this book, except for brief passages in reviews that refer to both author and publisher, may be reproduced without written permission of the publisher.

Illustrations and Design by: Gary J. Dolson

Library of Congress Catalog Card No. 81-83846
ISBN: 0-9607312-0-2

Published by: Personal Power Potential
 P.O. Box 693
 Wheeling, IL 60090

Introduction
BEYOND THE ROPE'S END

I LOVE AND FULFILLMENT
The Joy of Living   9
Just Let It Happen   13
Sex vs. Love   17
Self-Worth Determines Your Capacity for Love   21
Communicating with Those You Love   25
Love and Your Self-Image   31
Is Love a Risk?   35

II FINDING DIRECTION
Finding a Sense of Direction   39
How to Feel Sure of Yourself   43
Becoming a Whole Person   47
Time for Yourself   51
Checklist for Success   55
Don't Lose Your Individuality   59
Where Are You?   63

III SEX AND LIFE

Sexuality and Your Self-Esteem   67
Who's Playing Games - After Sex, What?   71
Must I Perform Again?   75
Why Men Are Sensitive About Sex   79
Sex and Social Success   83

IV GOING BEYOND YOUR COMFORT ZONE

The Risks of Growing   87
Making Decisions Under Pressure   91
The Death of a Relationship   95
Don't Be Afraid of Fear   99
How to Face Your Fears   103
Trusting Other People Again   107
What Constitutes a Drug Problem?   111
When Hope Is Gone   115

V EMOTIONAL SELF-RELIANCE

Emotional Self-Reliance 121
How to Deal With Hurt 125
Aloneness??? Loneliness??? 129
Introvert??? Extrovert??? 133
How to Survive One Day at a Time 137
Understanding Depression 141
What Do I Do with Anger? 145
How Do I Cope with Jealousy? 149
Weight Control and Your Ego 153

VI MAKING THE MOST OF MATURITY

Does Age Make a Difference? 159
Use It or Lose It 163
Sex After Sixty 167
What You See Is What You Get 171
The Conflicts of Aging 175

FOREWORD

By Karen M. Ross

"I've reached the end of my rope!!"
How often that expression is used—and sincerely felt. We feel we just can't hang on any longer . . . even that the end of the rope is out of reach.

The *end of the rope* is a different place for all of us. It may be as general as in everyday life—nothing seems to go right. It can be a specific decision making situation and the search for direction is difficult. Maintaining our self-esteem may need a boost. Sex is no longer a hush-hush subject so we can openly face some of the problems that can arise in this area of our lives.

Death, fear, hopelessness, depression, loneliness—all of these can cause great emotional discomfort. Survival can become a struggle. The natural aging process can create apprehension.

BEYOND THE ROPE'S END touches on all of these areas. In a clear, concise manner, a positive and enlightening answer to help you deal with your present confusion is offered.

Whatever your dilemma, Robert E. Ross will guide you BEYOND THE ROPE'S END.

Project your identity into the work of your hands. Some day you will go beyond the obvious. You will see your own reflection in your work, and you will know what is BEYOND THE ROPE'S END.

Introduction:
BEYOND
THE ROPE'S END

Did you ever feel that you were at the "end of your rope?" Someone will always say, "Just tie a knot and hang on." That sounds good, but it's not always that easy.

The Japanese have produced a new film, "The Dunes." The author portrays the journey of man through life somewhat like a modern Pilgrim's Progress. The traveler leaves the big city to find a meaningful life. He carries a pack and a large net to capture a creature that will bear his name and make him immortal. All day he searches. Night finds him weary and unfulfilled. The lonely desert offers no refuge. Suddenly he comes upon a stranger who offers him lodging for the night. He is guided to a deep sand pit. At the bottom is a small cabin. He descends on a rope ladder and enters the little house. Here he finds a woman who cooks and serves him a delicious meal, and shows him a place to sleep. The next morning he arises to leave and finds the rope ladder gone. He blames her for his plight. She informs him that the same thing happened to her first and now her life consists of sending up buckets of sand to her captor who sends down a bucket of food each day.

Angrily he charges the sand walls and they collapse under him. He tries to climb the rope when food is let down and unseen fingers release the rope and it falls to his feet.

With nothing left to do except cooperate, he sends up buckets of sand for a bucket of food and repeats the monotonous task. Finally he asks himself, "Do I move sand to live, or do I live to move sand?" He tries to escape, but finds himself right back where he started.

He keeps digging and one day discovers water. He watches the clear cool liquid form a pool. He looks in to see his own reflection and asks, "Is this the strange creature I came to find?" He sees himself reflected in his work and then looks up to find that the rope ladder has reappeared. He is now free to go, but he is not sure that he wants to leave the pit. He has found a reflection of himself in the toils of his life. Suddenly life has meaning. Fear is gone. New energy surges through his whole being.

Sometimes life seems to be an endless repetition of chores and limited rewards. We "shovel sand", debts pile up. Marriage fails; children get sick. The car needs repair; friends betray us. We get one problem solved, and confront yet another. We get one "bucket of food" for our effort and then we start all over.

It is not enough to share the earth with other forms of life, to just breathe and move about. We've paid a price to be more than a hungry creature of the sea or a roving animal on the earth. We want more, and we can have it. Sometimes we don't know what we want. The battle seems more important than its outcome.

There is only one thing that we really want from life; that is to know our beauty and worth as an individual. We want to be special and unique. We must see our own reflection in our work, and it is only then that we find fulfillment.

There is meaning beyond the rope's end. Let go of the

superficial. Don't worry over how much sand you moved or how many buckets of food you got for it. Look beyond your labor. Project your identity into the work of your hands. Some day you will go beyond the obvious. You will see your own reflection in your work, and you will know what is BEYOND THE ROPE'S END.

I

LOVE and FULFILLMENT

LOVE

There is no difficulty that enough love
    will not conquer;
No disease that enough love
    will not heal;
No door that enough love
    will not open;
No gulf that enough love will
    not bridge;
No wall that enough love will not
    throw down;
No sin that enough love
    will not redeem . . . .

It makes no difference How deeply
    seated may be the trouble,
How hopeless the outlook, How muddled
    the tangle, How great the mistake,
A sufficient realization of love will
    dissolve it all . . . .
If only you could love enough you
    would be the happiest and most powerful
    being in the world . . . .

    —Emmet Fox

THE JOY OF LIVING

The joy of living is yours if you will only accept it. Negative experiences cannot dampen your enthusiasm for life if you refuse to let them.

A young paralyzed college student was hailed by his classmates as the happiest and most optimistic student in school. He was elected student body president, and loved by all. A new student asked him about his illness and the young man replied, "I had polio." "How can you be so pleasant and happy, and still be paralyzed?" the new boy asked. "Well, the illness just touched my legs, not my heart," came the optimistic reply. Nothing will touch your heart without your permission.

Joy is a way of looking at life. A happy person looks at what he has, while the miserable soul bemoans what he "has not." Because of this negative appraisal of life, they live in poverty even though they may be rich in possessions. It is easy to mourn the loss of one coin, and miss the joy of having ninety-nine left.

Your attitude toward life is a matter of choice. There's a sign on a muddy country road: *"Choose your rut with care, you'll be in it for the next thirty miles."* This is true of attitude. Choose your attitude with care; it may guide you for the next thirty years. The joy of living is based on a positive attitude. It is seeing the good in your life no matter how dark a storm might be. Each flash of lightning will show you what is left to enjoy. Look at it.

Fulfillment brings joy in stages. Open your soul to the good around you. Let your eyes feast on the beauty of small details like raindrops and snowflakes. When you see one tree you also see a thousand leaves, and each has its own beauty and rewards to offer you. Look further and you will see the combined grandeur of rolling hills, lakes, forests, and magnificent mountains. These are all yours. They belong to the one who sees them. Every view is a joy, every sound is part of a symphony. Put them together and the experience is yours to keep.

The joy of living is waiting for you at the dawn of each new day. The sun comes up, the rooster blows his trumpet, the choir of birds . . . "Come Alive!" welcomes you to the festival of life. Make each day count whether you have a few of them or thousands at your disposal. Each hour is loaded with sixty minutes and each day with twenty-four hours. Neither fame nor fortune can change that for you. Your greatest fortune is to enjoy what God has given you, and to fill each hour with sixty minutes well spent. This could mean that you enjoy filling them with work, play, or love. You may just relax and take it easy. When did you last watch a sunset, listen to a song bird's melody of praise, or stop to smell the flowers? You need not miss the beauty, the melody, or the smell of nature.

The joy of living is yours if you will only stop, take a deep breath, and listen.

*Happiness is like a young colt
The more you chase him
The more he will elude you.
But if you turn your attention
    to other things,
He will come and nip you on
    your shoulder.*

JUST LET IT HAPPEN

The delicate relationship between man and woman cannot be rushed without losing the fine edge of spontaneity. To rush the progress of intimacy is to render it impersonal, and thereby destroy it. It becomes lost in the rush.

Our impatience affects our perspective. We look at things so differently when we are in a hurry. To watch a pot of water coming to boil doesn't increase the heat. It only seems to increase the time required for boiling. When you watch the hands of the clock they seem to move more slowly.

To prod and question a relationship will slow it down rather than contribute to its development. The prodding will interfere with the communication between the conscious and the subconscious mind.

The subconscious mind knows intuitively if a relationship has possibilities. A relaxed relationship permits the total person to get involved without fear. It allows the flow and movement of friendship to develop on many levels without interruption.

Too much prodding and pushing for more and more acts as a danger signal to the total person. The conscious mind is then alerted to questions and doubts. When pushed, we instinctively ask, "Why?", and one "why" leads to another. At this point the relationship is brought to a standstill for examination and reports. The conscious mind must now evaluate the "why" of every move, and reports must be filed away in memory. Now the attention is not on the fulfillment of the relationship, but on the analysis of events.

Some analysis is good, but too much dissipates emotion and leaves us cold. To analyze every word or act can lead to a paranoia which separates us from reality. A lack of awareness of the purpose in behavior of the other person can lead us into a foolish gullibility. The middle of the road will be different for each one of us, but very important. For the most part, good common sense will help us find it.

Relax, give the other person a chance to be as important as you wish to be. Focus your attention on honestly wishing for your partner all the joy and beauty which you desire for yourself. When you start programming yourself to fulfill the other person's happiness you become inspired with each success. Pretty soon you find yourself thrilled because they are thrilled, happy because they are happy, and fulfilled because they are fulfilled.

At this point you will find that you have climbed a mountain without effort, you have built a bridge without work. You have found that a meaningful relationship is yours without trying. It seems that you just let it happen.

Without love, sex becomes an empty echo on primitive drums telling the story of a lost treasure.

SEX vs LOVE

Sex is the "Song of God" vibrating on the tempered strings of man's soul. Its echo reverberates from earth to heaven bringing fulfillment to the divine image.

Without love, sex becomes an empty echo on primitive drums telling the story of a lost treasure.

Sex and Love can be opposites in the polarity of man's experiences, but together they produce a beam of light that dispels darkness. Together they produce a song that brings ecstatic joy. With love the song birds' strain is more melodious, and the golden hues of the setting sun take on added grandeur.

The beautiful combination of sex and love brings human ecstasy to the sublime pinnacle. The sexual experience moves from earth to heaven on the legacy of love. In Hemingway's *For Whom The Bell Tolls*, the old woman asks the young woman in love, "Did the earth move?" This is the quality of a relationship which brings certainty. It is the measure of 24 carat fine gold.

What we do about sex reveals our basic approach to life. It is more than an act. It is a magnetic phase of our personality which picks up demands to satisfy needs. If you are a taker, selfish and insecure, your sexual needs will demand pampering without concern for your partner. This type of sex precludes love. It is nothing more than receiving a bounty from another. If you are a mature, giving person who makes love a concomitant of sex, your greatest joy comes from the happiness of your partner.

Sex is a mirror which reflects our character and our maturity. Sexual fulfillment is an expression of personal need, but never at the expense of another's fulfillment or dignity. Through love one can experience superb joy by giving joy and ecstasy. In love we receive by giving.

The exotic significance of sex is not found in the act but in our appraisal of the act. The touch of a hand can be as electrifying as a kiss. One kiss could be orgasmic if appraised as such by the lover. The patterns of sexual fulfillment depend upon the values and responses of those involved.

Sexual preference is a unique expression of culture, education, values, and maturity. For this reason it is wise for lovers to consider these similar patterns in order to establish a lasting relationship. An attempt to mix cultural and educational patterns is often a cause of the brevity of some marriages.

Sex and love are not the same. They can exist together or separately. When sex dominates a relationship people become things rather than persons. They become controlled by their desire to hold onto their possession. They are free to express their personalities only within the limits established by this erotic relationship. One's likes and dislikes become a prison of one's own construction, making growth impossible.

When love dominates sex it becomes an experience of celebration. The sex act is an expression of a greater experience. It becomes an inexpressible experience which is both realistic and symbolic—both earthy and sublime.

Self-worth is developed by contributing to your world. Giving of yourself does not deplete the source, instead, it multiplies your assets in a unique way.

SELF-WORTH DETERMINES YOUR CAPACITY FOR LOVE

Your capacity for love is only limited by your immaturity and selfishness. Self-centered people do not have an adequate sense of self-worth. Their need for attention, and desire to be special are self-imposed limitations. Often a child is taught to be selfish by an insecure parent who worshipped the child for fear of losing the child's love.

The self-centered attitude starts in infancy. The baby is only aware of his own feelings and wants. All desire is translated into needs. The complaint with life will always be "it just doesn't meet my needs." If life permits, a child will remain a child forever. It all depends on how much a parent protected him from reality.

Self-worth cannot grow without the experience of giving. Self-worth must be felt in relation to one's ability to make a contribution to the lives of others. Finding your place in the world should be a normal process of dealing with reality. Life makes demands. You either meet them or lose the game. When one is protected from this danger one can't grow in spirit. The parent who gives and gives is expressing fear and insecurity. Their children are taught to be takers. They find their place in the world by receiving; so, they are constantly aware of their own needs. They can't be concerned with contributing. They have to receive to feel loved, and *never, never* do they know the joy of giving of themselves nor their hallowed possessions. Their friends are seen as a means to an end. Their family becomes an expression of their ego, and they feel rejected if the family doesn't pay dues to their selfishness.

Self-worth is developed by contributing to your world. Giving of yourself does not deplete the source, instead, it multiplies your assets in a unique way.

Self-worth and love walk hand in hand, constantly available for expression. Love has no selfish aim, no motive for giving, no desire for a pay off. Self-worth is the awareness that your knowledge, your work, your concern, your contribution can have meaning. It is this awareness that enables you to give without feeling loss. Self-worth goes beyond circumstances, opinions, or custom. It opens the door for love to be expressed. It is also the standard whereby love is measured.

When you realize that you are important to God Himself, you begin to feel the importance of your uniqueness. It is your uniqueness and singularity that makes your love special. You are special and your self-worth increases because there is a place for you. Now you can express love without fear. Your capacity to love is expanded by your ability to share.

Let go . . . give . . . expecting nothing in return and soon your capacity to give expands because you are a channel of love. God's love and energy flows through you. Your source, therefore, is never depleted.

In order to communicate, we must release our self-centered tendencies, and make a serious effort to understand those we love.

COMMUNICATING WITH THOSE WE LOVE

One of the most important factors in our lives is our communication system. It makes demands on us which cannot be ignored without suffering loss. We must release our self-centered tendencies, and make a serious effort to understand those we love. An exaggerated self-awareness can close in on you. You can become so aware of your breathing that every breath will come with great effort. You can become so aware of the process of going to sleep at night that you find sleep impossible.

You can become so aware of self and the world related to you that you can actually develop paranoia. To become paranoid means you begin to apply everything to yourself. A lady went to the racetrack and suddenly she was aware of her need for a safety pin. She turned to the lady next to her and asked, "Do you have a safety pin?" The lady said, "No, I don't." She turned to the lady on the other side and asked her, "Do you have a safety pin?" The lady said, "No, I really don't." She looked around and saw a lady behind her; as she started to ask for a safety pin, the voice on the loud speaker at the racetrack sounded, "They're off", and she fainted.

This is paranoia; an exaggerated self-awareness.

Another demand of good communication is this: if you are going to communicate with others you must put something extra into your relationship. It might be termed a "whizzle"— something extra. Did you ever go to a shoe shine parlor and have a boy shine your shoes? With every stroke he snaps the rag. The snap doesn't shine your shoes but it *gives you the feeling* he's doing a better job than the fellow who doesn't snap the rag. It's that snap, that "whizzle" that you put into your relationships that makes life meaningful. In your communication, it's the plus factor that you add. Others will be aware of it and glad that you're around to add a plus factor to their lives. To do this your communication must focus on their needs.

Another factor that will aid you in your communication will be your positive approach. We live in a world where people find so many reasons they cannot do the things they want to do. If your approach is positive, your faith increases. Faith is more a psychological term than it is a religious term. Actually, Jesus was the greatest psychologist that ever lived. He gave us many psychological factors which can simplify our lives tremendously; faith is the focal point of life. It's not basically a religious concept; it's the focal point of all mental activity. It is a psychological axiom that we move toward that on which our mind is focused. Focus on doubt and fear, you will move toward failure.

If we were to put a wooden beam across the floor, 30 feet long and a foot wide, you could step upon it and walk the full 30 feet. No problem; all would say, "That's easy." Now if that same beam were projected out the window to a building across the street, 20 floors above the pavement, it would change the whole picture. It's the same beam you just walked across, now let's see you walk from this building to the one across the street. You go to the window, you look out, you look down and you focus immediately upon the fact "I can't do it because I might fall." You focus on your fear, and at that point you say, "I can't." The very instant you forget your fear and focus on the fact that you have done it and that you can do it, it's a different ball game altogether. Research shows that failures have over 90% negative thoughts, and that successful people have 80% positive thoughts. What would happen to one who could activate 100% positive thinking? Faith is all in the way you look at it. It's your focal point that counts. Good communication is established through positive approach.

Another basic factor to effective communication is that we must be honest. This is sometimes difficult. If you're invited out to dinner and you don't like what is being served, you do not feel free to communicate your feelings. You can't always say what you want, or express what you feel. Being honest doesn't mean that you don't edit what you say. You don't say everything that comes to mind. Some people say, "Well, I just can't help it, I blurt out anything that comes to my mind." Nonsense! You know what you're saying and a part of you wants it said. You don't have to say everything that comes through your mind.

When you're communicating on a very serious item you should be honest. Children often help in making communications honest, and they will point it out when you are not totally honest. Dishonest parents just do not understand why their children will not listen to them. Parents will say, "Eat your spinach because it's good for you." The child's reaction is, if it's so good for me, why don't you eat yours? Quite logical! Some parents will teach their children to be honest, and yet communicate dishonesty. The child watches Dad when he gets change from buying gasoline; he gets $5.00 too much and he says, "Boy, I sure made a good deal on that one." The child goes away and begins to think in his mind, "Dad does it, why can't I?" Inconsistency in our non-verbal communication will cause conflict when we try to communicate something that's not quite accurate to children. Honesty is important, but edit what you say. You don't have to say everything you think.

Your self-image is determined by the focal point of your love. The direction of your love is a choice; the result is a destiny.

LOVE AND YOUR SELF-IMAGE

Love is a mirror that reflects your true image. Do you love things or people? Love of possessions reveals a shallow empty shell that cries out constantly to be filled. The emptiness plagues every solitary moment. Each passing hour is a search for something that will bring satisfaction. Each new possession will come and go leaving dissatisfaction in its path. There is no material thing that will satisfy a need that is spiritual. The love of possessions is a self-constructed restraint which holds one back from fulfillment. The self-image is one of weariness and boredom.

The love of physical stimulation, based on alcohol or chemicals, creates an exhaustion from decreasing returns. One high soon runs its course. Then more and more highs are needed to feel the intensity of the last one. The search moves from the simple to the complex. At first the sensations are purely physical. Just one drink produces the feeling of relaxation and freedom. Then two are needed for the same experience. Soon the number grows and grows into a deceptive monster. As the body gets weaker the high promises false fulfillment. The strength decreases as the drinks increase. Then comes the complex conclusions. "Let's get high, and be somebody." As one indulges his desire for physical stimulation he keeps saying, "It doesn't make sense, but I know what I feel." The first part is true," It doesn't make sense," and the second part is false, "I know what I feel." As the drinks increase, the feelings become more and more disguised. The body plays games, and the mind becomes blurred to reality. The love of physical stimulation produces a confused self-image as reality fades out of sight. The love of praise can be the most dangerous of all. To be loved for what we produce is not being loved as a person. The praise and admiration of others is beautiful but can be as dangerous as a serpent. This need is very costly. It can exhaust the resources of the strong. It will challenge the wisdom of the most daring. Fools risk their lives for applause. They express their personal joy of praise, but the echo soon dies to leave an ugly void. The love of praise reflects a shallow image of an unfulfilled destiny.

To love another person is to rise to a higher plane of joy. To see the worth of a soul is to see with divine perspective. It is then important to protect the dignity of others, even our defeated enemies. At the close of World War II, General Eisenhower was to conduct the surrender of the German army. Just before the start of the ceremony, a newsman asked him, "What are you thinking about at this time?" General Eisenhower's comment was an indication of greatness as he said, "I must accept his surrender and yet protect his dignity." *If we love others, we will protect their dignity whether we win or lose.* Your love of others will produce an image of greatness.

The most noble image of all is manifest in our love of God. God is Love. To love Him creates a unique image of peace and satisfaction. The human soul can only be happy with the possibility of endless growth, and this is the only self-image that is totally acceptable.

Your self-image is determined by the focal point of your love. The direction of your love is a choice; the result is a destiny.

Loving is making a deal with life—where it is impossible to lose.

IS LOVE A RISK?

Love is never a risk; that is, love in the highest sense. Eros is always a risk, friendship is always a risk, but never true love. You may ask, "What if I love and my love is not returned?" That is very possible in the experience of love. Genuine love need not be returned in order to be experienced. Since true love is its own reward, the experience of love transforms the individual to a higher level of existence. Life is made up of vibrations of energy—all of us vibrate on different frequencies; also, we vibrate on different levels at different stages of our lives—and we move from the lower to the higher levels through the experience of love.

Love is so powerful that you are elevated by the experience of loving, and the one receiving your love is elevated even in the absence of their reciprocation.

Loving is making a deal with life—where it is impossible to lose. Love generates energy, and you can become tireless in your efforts to express love for someone else. This is expressed in the picture of Father Flanagan's Boys Town, depicting one little boy carrying another on his back, and his statement is, "He ain't heavy, Father, he's my brother."

Love makes heavy loads lighter by generating within the heart, soul, and body of the lover more strength, more energy, more endurance.

Love gives, not demanding anything in return. Love is the essence of kindness, love generates patience even in the impulsive. Love enables one to suffer without feeling pain; to experience lack without feeling deprived. Love transcends time and space and reaches out to the beloved, and yet, in the presence of the beloved, time ceases to exist. Hours seem like fleeting moments.

> *"For Those Who Love Time Is Not"*
>
>   *Time is*
> *Too slow for those who Wait,*
> *Too swift for those who Fear*
> *Too long for those who Grieve,*
> *Too short for those who Rejoice;*
> *But for those who Love*
>   *Time is Not.*
>
>   *Author Unknown*

The only risk in loving is separation anxiety. Separation anxiety is not a loss; it is not something taken from us, it is an emotion that we create to deal with losses that we feel are unpleasant. The absence of one that we love is a loss, but the anxiety is our own creation. Even love in absence has meaning and power. Yet, as time heals all wounds, it also diminishes desire, and brings freedom to establish new relationships. Thus, in time, the heart that loves rises to love again.

II

FINDING DIRECTION

If you wish to change your sense of direction—change your focal point. Whatever catches your eye catches you.

FINDING A SENSE OF DIRECTION

When you move toward becoming a better you, you know that you are moving in the right direction.

Make it your goal to become better in every way every day of your life. This can be done by repeating an affirmation hourly for only fifteen seconds. The following affirmation will work:

> *I thank God that in my life I experience Abundance, Health, Wealth, Strength, Wisdom, Knowledge, Harmony, Love, Opulence, Laughter, Joy, and Peace.*

Don't analyze it, don't pick it apart. Just affirm it. Your first reaction may be, "I don't have all of those things." Change that to say, "I don't have them to the degree that I want them." If you possess as little as 10% of each, you possess a start. Your continued repetition of this affirmation will insure an increase in each attribute. As days pass you will know you are moving in the right direction.

To evaluate your sense of direction test yourself with the following question:

> *If I were to give up everything in my life but one thing, what would I cling to? If I were to give up all ideals and values but one, what would it be?*

To realize what ideal is most significant to you if you were to give up all others gives you your starting point. Now you know where to begin. The direction we take is determined by our *focal point of desire*. When we visualize this point we move toward it. Whatever we desire greatly, we think about and thus our focal point draws us as a moth to a flame.

If you wish to change your sense of direction—change your focal point. Whatever catches your eye catches you. Your imagination is far more powerful than your intellect. Your intellect can evaluate your goal, but your imagination will determine your direction toward it.

If your sense of direction is to bring personal fulfillment, you must understand your value system and use it as a compass. Many unhappy people are motivated by another's values. They permit others to set the pace, and they become influenced by values that lack meaning to them. Thus their unhappiness is inevitable. You will find that comparing yourself with others, or being in competition with others is a self-defeating trap. Your sense of direction must come from within.

No one can ever fulfill you except you, and your fulfillment is impossible without taking the risk of growing.

The purpose of growing is to become better. You must accept your life as a gift, and accept the responsibility of acting in your own best interest. If you don't, you will hold others responsible for your life by demanding appreciation, fulfillment, and a sense of completeness by proxy.

The first step in finding direction is to believe that you are a good person, and that what you seek is good, providing you are honest. Goodness may not be what you have been, but it can be where you are going from today on. Forget the failures of the past and start from here—today.

Your visualization of a good outcome will help you to feel sure of yourself, and your new feeling will help produce the positive result. The power of positive pictures produces a powerful effect in the subconscious mind which changes ideas into reality.

HOW TO FEEL SURE OF YOURSELF

When negative experiences produce doubt and fear in your mind, you may find it difficult to feel sure of yourself. Difficult, but you can do it.

The first step is a decision to have more positive experiences. To carry this off repeat your commitment as often as you can. Emile Coue developed a therapy based on autosuggestion. People still laugh at his famous sentence, "Day by day, in every way, I am getting better and better." He did not claim to cure anybody, but those who wanted to be healed and have a better life tried his remedy, and it worked. Why did it work? There is power in repeated words. Self-induced changes can be brought about by repeated phrases. When they are repeated often enough they generate emotional energy. Emotional energy always produces change.

Whatever you repeat often enough you will come to believe. It will become a part of you. This is the basis of the famous creed that: "Whatever the mind can conceive and believe, it can achieve." There are many analytical people who say, it's impossible or it won't work. Sure enough, if that is their belief it won't work for them. They have no problem with it.

The reason it doesn't work for these analytical people is their constant internal dialogue. The internal dialogue will keep reminding them of past negative experiences, problems, and failures.

To feel sure of yourself you must stop this internal dialogue which causes depression and fear. To stop it you must first tune in and listen. If this internal dialogue is filled with negative, depressing thoughts, the outcome will be failure. The slowdown of depressive thought must be countered with plans for action. If you play a fast game of table tennis, you will change both your physical and emotional rhythm, and block the negative internal dialogue.

Look for the humor in your problem, and it will help you to feel sure that it will come out okay. If six things go wrong with your car, laugh at the seventh. You will be amazed at how little it will bother you when you laugh. The laughter will stop the negative internal dialogue.

Visualize a positive outcome for any event you face, and you will feel sure of yourself. Your proposed vision will generate emotional and physical energy. When you argue, using logic and facts, you are functioning with the left hemisphere of your brain which doesn't produce emotional reactions—just facts. Visualization moves the mental process to the right hemisphere where it produces energy and physical sensations. For example: pretend you have a lemon in your hand, feel its texture, now smell it, lay it on a board and cut it, watch the juice run out. Visualize this for a few minutes and you will experience an increase in the flow of saliva in your mouth. Your imagination did it all. It produced a vision, it produced energy, it produced a sensation. Your visualization of a good outcome will help you feel sure of yourself, and your new feeling will help produce the positive result. The power of positive pictures produces a powerful effect in the subconscious mind which changes ideas into reality.

Becoming a whole person is a lifetime process of moving toward fulfillment. First it is necessary to choose a destiny, and then you can plan a road map of interesting stops on your way. This destiny must reach beyond time and space.

BECOMING A WHOLE PERSON

"Is this all there is?" is so often asked by those feeling the emptiness of an unfulfilled life. Too much time is spent searching for that moment of exhilaration. Every effort is made to have fun. Good times are measured in terms of fun, but when it is past there is a void. Fun is good for you, but it takes more to bring fulfillment. Today's trend is to find a tensionless existence. Even that goal can leave life boring and meaningless.

Becoming a whole person is a lifetime process of moving toward fulfillment. First it is necessary to choose a destiny, and then you can plan a road map of interesting stops on your way. This destiny must reach beyond time and space.

In moving toward fulfillment there is a letting go of the things that don't really count. Excess baggage will always impede progress. Take the little things in stride. Mountains can become mole hills if you refuse to let the process reverse itself. Sometimes a heartfelt, "So what!" will handle the little irritating events that could create rough edges in your experience. Indifference becomes a virtue when applied to the little unpleasantries of life.

Decide what is really important to you and pursue it with all your might. If you hold it in your vision, you can't help but move toward it. A whole person chooses his direction, and with patience moves that way. The opinions of others will not make you whole; so don't live by them. If others control your life with their criticism, you will never please them nor yourself. Recognition, prestige, importance, approval, status, and respect of others are all by-products and never a goal within themselves. These privileges only come to the one with independence of personality, one who develops self-confidence and adequacy by moving toward the goals of usefulness and creativity.

Solve your own problems if you possibly can. Each time you accept the challenge you grow a little more. With each success you can tackle a bigger problem, and in this way you develop your own self-esteem. Self-esteem is the feeling that you can face life head-on and solve any problem life presents to you. As your self-esteem grows you become a whole person.

Seek out people you can admire. It will help you to become a whole person. If you love life and love yourself, the best way to perpetuate that growth is to share it with someone whom you feel to be your equal. When you admire a friend, don't look up to them. Look straight across at them as equals, not superiors. If you see them as superior, your feelings of inferiority will impede your progress to become a whole person. By the same token, if you only associate with those to whom you feel superior, your pride will retard your growth.

It is good to be creative in your work, but it is also important to take time for recreation. Play is not condemned if it is *recreative,* but when it occupies excessive time and consumes your life you miss the whole person concept.

Decide to enjoy every phase of life possible. Diminish the

effect of irritations. Accept the challenge of life's problems with a positive attitude. Allow yourself to experience pleasure without guilt. Move toward your chosen goals with determination and you will become a whole person.

Take Time to think—It is the source of power
*Take Time to play—It is the secret of
  perpetual youth*
Take Time to read—It is the fountain of wisdom
*Take Time to pray—It is the greatest power
  on earth*
*Take Time to love and be loved—It is a God-
  given privilege*
*Take Time to be friendly—It is the road to
  happiness*
Take Time to laugh—It is the music of the soul
*Take Time to give—It is too short a day to
  be selfish*
Take Time to work—It is the price of success
*Take Time to do charity—It is the key to
  heaven.*
—Author Unknown

TIME FOR YOURSELF

Individuals who feel driven by *time* and by *others* are headed for serious trouble. They limit themselves in the joys of life where the real living takes place.

A hiker came upon a man fishing, and stopped to watch him. The fisherman tugged at his line and pulled a large trout, examined it and threw it back into the water. Then he pulled in a large perch, unhooked it and threw it back also. Next he caught a small fish, put it into his pouch and started to leave. The hiker asked why he threw back the big fish and kept the small ones. "Small frying pan," replied the fisherman.

Too many people limit their capacity to be creative and enjoy life. They just don't have time for the experiences that count. One can throw back the really big ones, and focus on small details that rob life of valuable time to do real living.

The compulsive person wants to do what is right, but puts too much emphasis on unimportant details. Some accounting specialists will waste thirty dollars worth of time to find a thirty cent mistake.

The ability to work with detail is good. It is a personality characteristic which will enable one to be effective in his chosen field. If that characteristic is employed when it is not needed it becomes a crutch. It inhibits freedom when carried as a security device. If you find personal gratification in perfecting unnecessary detail, your life can be used up on the unimportant. Friends will find you picky and unpleasant. They will be irritated with this emphasis on the insignificant.

Take time to enjoy life. Live one day at a time. When you've done all you can to resolve a problem move on to a new experience. Living is too important to be wasted on useless brooding.

Life is also too beautiful to be used up on constant work, work, work. The workaholic works to satisfy an emotional need—the need to be busy. To be busy is not always to be productive. Excessive work may actually cut one's productiveness.

Take time out from worry. The worrier worries when nothing is wrong. To be free from worry you must change your focus. Look up! You will feel better when you see the sky. You will then see more to life than the stones at your feet.

A change of focal point can change your destiny. Focus on being a healthy, whole person, and beyond that—relax and let life take its course. The universe is under control.

A creative and productive individual enjoys his work and is willing to share its beauty, but needs no approval from others to know that it is good.

CHECKLIST FOR SUCCESS

Success does not exist in reality. It is only an idea—a measure of competition and comparison. If measured in dollars, it loses value as the economy moves. If measured in results of your labor, nothing is permanent in time. If success is measured by your superiority to others, it is lost when you meet one who is above you. To the success conscious person there is no joy in the process of moment to moment living, since life is regarded only as a means to an end.

Thousands of years ago the Bhagavad Gita spoke against the evil of working for rewards:

> *You have the right to work but for work's sake only. You have no right to the fruits of work. Desire for the fruits of work should never be your motive in working ... Renounce attachment to the fruits ... Work done with anxiety about results is far inferior to work done without such anxiety in the calm of self-surrender. They who work selfishly for results are miserable.*

One is successful in life when one's work can be enjoyed as an end in itself. When the task becomes its own reward we are free from fear and anxiety about our job. Fear is only a shadow cast by ambition to be recognized as greater than we really are. To be free from fear we must let go of goals aimed at winning rewards and recognition.

If success means that you must feel better than others, then pride dominates your value system. This produces hostility and anger because it grows out of the fear that others may actually be better than you. Pride is a leaning attitude which needs the support of the opinion of others.

A creative and productive individual enjoys his work and is willing to share its beauty, but needs no approval from others to know that it is good.

Your checklist for genuine success is not based on what others may think, but on the following:

> Is it good?
> Is it creative?
> Does it serve a purpose?
> Do I enjoy it?
> Does it bring something to someone?
> Does it have meaning?

If your answers are affirmative, your checklist for success is not measured by others, nor is it affected by the approval of others. At this point it can never be taken from you.

*Neither a borrower nor a lender be;
For loan oft loses both itself and friend,
And borrowing dulls the edge of husbandry.
This above all: to thine own self be true,
And it must follow, as the night the day,
Thou canst not then be false to any man.*

—William Shakespeare

DON'T LOSE YOUR INDIVIDUALITY

"He'll never change," and "Why should he?" is a direct expression of the futility of trying to make over a companion. Basically, it is true that people never change. Basic assumptions about life remain the same, but we do change our methods of expressing them. In this way we seem to change, but our goals remain quite stable.

A controlling personality may change methods or timing, but will seek control on different levels. When one technique fails they will change to another, but this is not a change in personality. One can change from cruel to kind, or from sour to sweet without changing basic goals. They will at times twist meanings in order to maintain control, but in twisting the meanings of a relationship one avoids reality. If we have a neurotic need to be right, we must deal in half truths, and misplaced meanings. This is cheating at life's game. If one cheats it is easy to win, but there is a feeling of emptiness when we win a phoney victory.

Changes in values, relationships, and interests are necessary for personal growth. Equitable relationships demand flexibility, but not changes in personality. We do not have the right to change others, or make over a companion, but we can project what we feel is important to us in the relationship. Don't give up because you don't see changes instantly; minute changes may take years to surface and become obvious. We make changes slowly because the established patterns of life give us a feeling of ease. We feel secure in doing things as we always did them.

Why change? You don't change as long as your techniques are getting the results you want. But when one is depressed, unhappy, and unfulfilled it is time to make changes. Sometimes an incidental change will produce magnificent results. A cheerful "Good Morning" can change a day's trend, and thus change its ending.

Many good relationships are lost because of an extreme either-or attitude. "Either do it my way or don't do it." Sometimes tolerance is a measure of success. Gray areas are necessary to make life into a pleasing picture—all black or white is harsh and cold. Tolerant people find that they are not as far apart as circumstances would imply. Rigidity creates distance without bridges.

Changes are difficult, but not impossible. It is natural to resist change. If the temperature goes up we perspire to keep cool; if it goes down we shiver to increase our warmth. Nature's trend is no changes. Yet, life demands it on all sides.

We must decide what we want out of life, and then make only the changes necessary to get it without losing our integrity and our value system. It is far better to be alone and without friends than to purchase such at the price of our personal worth. Hang on to your individuality at any cost—it is the only lasting and meaningful value you will ever have.

*North, South, East, West,
all Roads lead to fulfillment.
It all depends upon how you
handle each milestone.
The measure of a man is
how he bears up under misfortune.*

WHERE ARE YOU?

Where are you living in relation to life's significant values? You may ask, "Who decides what is significant?" You do! You make all of the decisions in your life. Even the decision to cooperate with a decision which contradicts your values. You are where you are by choice.

Your development at this point in time determines your reactions to any given situation. Your anger today is far different from that of ten years ago. Words or actions that would have angered you then may go unnoticed today, or the reverse may be true. Your anger can tell you where you are now.

What's funny to you? Your laughter and sense of humor is identifying your location on the road to maturity. A humorous situation to one person may arouse disgust in another. Your disgust and your humor identify you very distinctly, and indicate where you are.

Your territorial imperatives locate you very precisely. Farmers have been killed because of insisting that a field fence be moved two feet. Nations move into the wrong territory and war erupts. Are you threatened symbolically when someone crosses your yard? Do you respond like a growling dog or a potential friend? We watch your response to invasion, and estimate, "Well, that's where you are right now."

Your concept of people tells a great deal about your progress. Do you treat a person as a thing or an equal entity? If all of your relationships are "I—it," you have a long journey ahead of you. Also, do you respond like an *it* when someone seeks your friendship? If you would have friends, you must prove yourself friendly.

Your courage reveals your location. Courage is based on your values. We fight for right. We stand for principle, and take risks in proportion to our place in the world. Our great nation once fought over the ownership of slaves. There were some who believed slavery was good depending on where they were in their development. The strength of each man's conviction gave him the courage to choose his flag and fight for its symbolic meaning.

Your tolerance is a revelation of your development. If someone disagrees with you, it does not mean that one of you must be wrong. It just means that he or she is not where you are right now. Two people can disagree and both be right. It just depends upon perspective, and your perspective is determined by where you are. If you feel that the thoughts of another are absurd, you can accept or reject those thoughts by knowing, "Well, that's just where you are right now."

Look not with disdain upon those who seem ridiculous to you. Maybe that's where you were a few months or years ago.

III

SEX and LIFE

Ego strength and sexual fulfillment move on the same wave length. Each is enhanced by the other. A good self-image is a beginning point toward sexual fulfillment, and that fulfillment builds the self-image.

SEXUALITY AND YOUR SELF-ESTEEM

Some find it impossible to permit the ego to get involved in the sexual relationship. Males struggle with this issue more than females. Men often prefer an impersonal concept of sex. Some fear that the female will rob them of more than is just. Freud called it a fear of castration. The male is frightened of being consumed by the female.

The female seems more dangerous than the male, sexually, because she takes the relationship more seriously. She does so because it pervades her whole life. Her sexuality begins with her dress and appearance. It goes beyond fulfillment in copulation. Her sexuality reaches into pregnancy, childbirth, breast feeding, child care, and on to watch the child graduate to success as an adult.

The consequences of there being two sexes are far greater for women than for men. Women's sexuality is long term and men's is the opposite. The burden is usually placed upon the woman's shoulders for success or failure sexually. This is illogical when we realize that sexual fulfillment tends to bind the woman and sever the man from a relationship, temporarily. Following sexual involvement, the woman wants to hold on, and the man wants to let go for a while. The difference is difficult for both to understand. The man interprets her as being possessive and controlling; the woman interprets his behavior as rejection. This difference has always existed, and has usually been ignored. A woman appears illogical because her emotional life reaches into every avenue of her being. She may color her whole life with the feeling of one event. The male will not understand this because it does not fit his pattern. The male pattern is to fragment his life, and keep it compartmentalized.

Men fail to understand women because of the ambivalence of emotion. A woman can answer yes and no to the same question and be honest in her answer. Her ability to feel more gives strength to her ego, but confusion to her male companion.

The source of renewal for the female differs from the male. The expression of concern and endearment is meaningful to a woman, but might cause a male to feel less masculine if he is insecure. We all want to be loved, but men often pretend that they can get along without it. It is possible that an expression which may cause a woman to feel better may cause the male to feel dependent. He will then reject it and not be understood by the female. Some have difficulty enjoying sex because they feel that they are unworthy creatures. The weakened ego looks upon himself as so undeserving that he dare not permit even the thought of sexual pleasure.

Historically, the Christian church has generally misinterpreted the significance of sexual fulfillment, and condemned any feelings of sexual pleasure. In an attempt to scorn earthly life, the church has expressed an intense hostility to pleasure, and above all, sexual pleasure. Many feel that the body is a prison in which the soul is trapped, that it is the body that drags the soul down to sin, and that the quest for pleasure is wrong; especially sexual pleasure. They forget that sex was God's idea to start with, and He reminds us: "Call not that which I have made unclean."

One purpose of sexuality is to strengthen the ego or elevate self-esteem. The vibrations of the mind and ego are elevated by the sexual fulfillment of the body. One good orgasm is worth more than a full bottle of tranquilizers.

Ego strength and sexual fulfillment move on the same wave length. Each is enhanced by the other. Sexuality acts as a carrier wave to the communication system between the sexes. A good self-image is a beginning point toward sexual fulfillment, and that fulfillment builds the self-image.

Take time to express your sexuality. Let it begin in the primary areas of cleanliness, dress, and perfume or aftershave. When you are clean and neat you feel like holding your head a little higher, and it is easier to feel secure with the opposite sex.

Your gradual expression, without risking anything, will keep you on safe ground. Move carefully into the territory of the other person, and soon you will find you are welcome. Your ease in expression will increase with your confidence, and the feeling of being sexual will increase your confidence.

When you suppress the true expression of your personal desires it prevents their ultimate realization. Your game of "escape responsibility" also becomes a trap to prevent self-realization.

WHO'S PLAYING GAMES—AFTER SEX WHAT?

It's difficult to let the world know that you want to be loved. If you do, you may be misinterpreted as being promiscuous, or rejected as immature. In an effort to get the message across and yet appear not to, it is easy to start playing games.

Without being aware, it is possible to identify with someone who expresses your feelings in part, and thus you are not responsible for the expression. This denial of responsibility also prevents you from tapping your own resources and developing your growth. When you suppress the true expression of your personal desires it prevents their ultimate realization. Your game of "escape responsibility" also becomes a trap to prevent self-realization, and saves you from taking chances.

Conscience is a game that eats into the mind to destroy from within. It is established by culture and prejudice. Conscience is a battle between our success mechanism and our failure mechanism. Our goal to win acceptance as a child caused us to accumulate a list of rules and regulations. These rules have no bearing upon our worth as a person, but if we think they do, we are trapped. It can become a game of escape: "My conscience won't let me reach fulfillment." Now we have an excuse for failure, and a technique for appearing to be righteous.

A list of rules and regulations is an over simplification of conscience. No list of rules can be long enough to bring peace. You can obey every rule you know, and still degrade yourself in an attempt to satisfy conscience. The only answer to conscience is to accept forgiveness by forgiving yourself. Refuse to worry about every little thing that might happen. Refuse to hate yourself for every little fault. If you permit conscience to tyrannize you, you will not see your opportunities for full living. When conscience makes unreasonable demands of you and crushes positive feelings, it becomes a tool of evil and not a message from God.

Conscience is a game to avoid intimacy, and false guilt over sex is one way to prevent sexual fulfillment from leading to intimacy. Sex is an excellent avenue to intimacy, but easily avoided with the disguise of righteousness. Who would criticize you for wanting to be righteous? The game is endless in subtle platitudes and false ideals. Is it bad to touch the hand, the arm, the face, the back, the stomach of the opposite sex? Your conscience may tell you—"Not unless you enjoy it. If it is stimulating sexually, it must be immoral." How ridiculous can your conscience get?

Your self-image is your guiding star. It is your self-image which drives you on to success, or drags you down to failure. It is your concept of yourself and your self-worth that determines your feelings toward other people and, for the most part, their feelings toward you. Your sexuality is a part of all this. Let yourself be sexual without guilt, and your self-image will improve.

After sex you can feel fulfilled if you accept it as a good in your life. It is related to your desire to be loved, if experienced with respect for your dignity as well as your partner's. There is no reason for depression to follow a sexual involvement unless you need that game to protect you from your fear of intimacy.

Remember sexuality does not subtract from your total assets. Paradoxical as it may seem, when you give of yourself you receive. Your self-image is elevated. Depression following sex is an implication that you now feel less than you were. This can only be true when you feel that the person involved is far beneath you, or has values which conflict with yours.

Accept your sexuality as a means of enlarging your self-esteem through an unselfish act of personal gratification and this paradox opens for you a personality expression which can only bring a feeling of fulfillment and joy.

"Performance only" is usually the result of the loss of admiration. The admiration that two people have for each other will provide the strength to weather the storms which are sure to come.

MUST I PERFORM AGAIN?

Sexual performance by itself is prostitution. It doesn't make much difference to your feelings whether you are paid in money, food, clothing, or satisfaction of duty. You still feel the same. You feel cheap when asked to perform without personal respect. The impersonal quality of an empty performance becomes little more than a business deal.

When the sex act is an empty performance it loses the beauty of spontaneity. It is little more than masturbation. It puts sex in the category of any other appetite. Sex is a normal appetite, but different than any other in that it can elevate or debase the human spirit. Our cultural teachings have cast an aura of mystery and morality around sexuality. It is this aura that produces the negative emotional effects of the sexual experience.

The purpose of sex has been misinterpreted. It has become a lever to dominate the cultural dogmas of nearly every race in the world. Its most significant purpose is the elevation of the human spirit, but when reduced to the "performance only" level it loses that impact.

Performance can be an expression of pride. It can demonstrate physical strength and express excitement like no other experience of humanity. Even on its lower level of "performance only" sex is the strongest driving force of the natural world. When the fullest expression on this level is reached we still want more. We want to realize the full potential of what we sense to be potentially more than just another gratification.

The feeling "must I perform again" is a sure sign that the relationship between two people is deteriorating. When you feel it, it is time to reevaluate. It is time to recapture the significant values that brought you together or all will be lost.

Performance can become a testing technique to produce reassurance. The sad part is that it fails to do so. One who lives on reassurance, knowing that it is false, is expressing a sense of inferiority. He or she is willing to settle for less than his or her worth.

"Performance only" is usually the result of the loss of admiration. Even though sexual passion is important it cannot sustain a couple across a lifetime. It cannot provide sufficient support for the weight carried by a continuing relationship. The admiration that two people have for each other will provide the strength to weather the storms which are sure to come. The reclaiming of admiration is necessary in order to lift the sexual relationship above the "performance only" syndrome. The word syndrome is applicable since it refers to a group of symptoms describing a disease. The "performance only" relationship is in a state of ill health. The only cure is to reclaim heartfelt admiration which is the beginning point of romantic love.

He must realize that man and woman are not enemies, but the dogmatic definitions of masculinity and femininity are enemies.

WHY MEN ARE SENSITIVE ABOUT SEX

Being a boy is particularly hazardous during childhood. There are cultural pressures on the boy to be traditionally masculine, more so than on girls to be feminine. If a girl is a tomboy, she is cute. If a boy is a sissy, he is degraded to shame and rejection.

In today's culture boys have few men around enough of the time to teach them how to be a man. When Dad is home he is busy or watching the ball game. The boy is left with nearly all female authority figures. His mother cares for him at home. Chances are great that his elementary teacher will be female. Consequently, the boy has to learn to identify himself as a man by what he hears, reads, or sees on TV. These concepts of masculinity are often confusing and misleading. Most boys grow up not really knowing how to "act like a man." Father's role is often that of the punisher when he is home, and this creates a *negative identification* with men. He is taught that "real boys" are active and strong, and then he gets into trouble at school when he acts like a "real boy." He is in constant conflict with his desire to be active and his teachers' desire that he be quiet, submissive, and passive. His logical conclusion is that to be acceptable, he must act feminine.

Boys are often taught not to feel. If he gets hurt, he is encouraged to deny his pain because "big boys don't cry." It's okay for girls to cry, but for a boy it is humiliation. As he moves into adolescence he learns that the hero of a ball game is the one who continues to play after he is hurt. Society says "tune out your body—ignore your feelings" if you want to be a real man.

Emotional problems are foolishly ignored in the world of the "real man." Men resist seeking professional help so they will not appear weak. This concept is magnified to include all emotion. Many men find it difficult to give honest expression to love and gentleness.

Fear of the rejection of his masculinity causes many men to avoid intimacy. The confusion about masculinity and femininity in a changing world has put tremendous sexual pressures on both men and women. To the male a sexual identity is more momentous than to the female. To be a man he must be a competent "performer" always ready to show how good he is. Consequently, it is safer for the fearful male not to get too close to a female. Intimacy seems dangerous because more may be demanded of sex than can be produced.

Men can solve their sensitivity about sex by realizing that the role learned in childhood to satisfy parents and society, is an ultimate denial of self. To live in that role is to live with symbols that never satisfy. He must realize that man and woman are not enemies, but that the dogmatic definitions of masculinity and femininity are enemies. To withdraw from competition between the sexes is to find fulfillment in the relationship.

For a man to accept himself and females as persons, and

not as rigid symbols, is a step toward sexual confidence. Be a person first and nothing can force you to be something you do not elect to be. Also, this is the open door for you to become free and able to express yourself without fear.

Social success and sexuality must be viewed within the framework of your value system. Any social relationship which leaves you feeling less than you want to be is never social success.

SEX AND SOCIAL SUCCESS

Social success and sexual relationships are sometimes erroneously thrown together. It is a common game for some men to convince a female that there is only one way to make it in this competitive world—she must pay off sexually. Any man who uses this technique to win a sexual involvement is expressing his feelings of sexual inadequacy. This technique is saying: "I'm willing to buy what my personality can't earn." It is also the male's way of keeping sexuality on an impersonal level. It is prostitution when a man feels that his personal responsibility to his partner ends with a gift or a payment. When a man feels this impersonal attitude toward his wife he sees her as a leech because her material needs reach into months and years of dependency. He accepts her dependency when he wants her, and rejects it when he is satisfied. This is the impersonal attitude of those who fear intimacy.

All men are not alike. It is impossible to interpret behavior without some knowledge of the character of the persons involved. Two people with identical behavior could have motives which are worlds apart. One who is acquainted with puppies and has never met a rattlesnake might misinterpret the friendly gesture of a wagging tail. Also, it creates limitations in relationships to infer that all gestures of friendliness will result in venomous consequences.

The sexual difference between male and female is your most important consideration if you desire an equitable relationship with the opposite sex. Our culture has ignored, denied, suppressed, and distorted woman's sexuality according to the needs of the moment, and everybody is puzzled and dissatisfied with the results. Females are taught to squelch sexual feelings, and to withdraw from a relationship when they feel "turned on." If they decide to marry, they are then expected to automatically reverse this former indoctrination. If they find this difficult, we condemn them as the cause for any emotional failure in the marriage. This cultural problem can produce confusion in the most intelligent. This confusion makes social success difficult.

A woman should not ignore the fact that she finds fulfillment in being sexually attractive. This is the beginning of the long term concept of sexuality. It begins with the way she looks. This is important because she communicates with her appearance. A woman can be attractive and modest indicating that her relationships are selective. She walks with pride and the whole world knows that she is proud to be a female. Also, a woman can be well-dressed and immodest, communicating that she is available to most any male. A woman can be socially successful and not be sexually available.

Social success and sexuality must be viewed within the framework of your value system. Any social relationship which leaves you feeling less than you want to be is never social success.

IV

GOING BEYOND YOUR COMFORT ZONE

*Every person has a mountain to climb.
For one it may be weakness—
    for another it may be strength.
For one it may be fame—
    for another obscurity.
Whatever your mountain you must climb
    it to find fulfillment.*

THE RISKS OF GROWING

Growth demands changes. It is necessary to give up views and customs that no longer seem appropriate. To cling to unreal views of life makes growing impossible. Yet to give them up is threatening. What will replace your discarded convictions? Will the new be better than the old? Is this the way to find happiness? These risks must be taken if one is to grow.

Growth means to fill the gap between what you have been and what you want to be. What you have been is familiar, and with the familiar you feel secure. It is not easy to let go of secure feeling, but it is worth it to become better.

To start, you must take the risk of being yourself. No other risk is quite so fearful, and yet none is so easy to maintain. If you can't be yourself, you never learn what life is all about. To be yourself you must ignore what others may think of you. If you have to be false to get approval, you live in an unreal world. You are *taking* the risk of missing life in order to *avoid* the risk of an unfavorable opinion. Real prestige is never built upon false esteem.

In order to grow you may have to risk your reputation. When life demands performance of you the experience will provoke questions in your thoughts and feelings:

> *Did I do well?*
> *Did I do my best?*
> *Did I make mistakes?*
> *How far did I fall short?*
> *Will they think I'm good?*

These are common questions which can prod you on to new horizons of progress. If you are to grow, these risks are inevitable.

Growing will expose you to the possibility of being wrong or even total failure occasionally. To grow you must have the courage to face your imperfections and polish them until they become assets. There is the risk of being misunderstood and rejected in the process. Don't let it startle you because those who reject you at this time are only expressing their own imperfections. Relax and give them an opportunity to grow, too. When they've grown they will come back, and if they don't grow you're better off if they don't return. As you grow you will change your circle of friends. And that circle will grow as you grow.

Growth is always worth the risk. Without it one never knows the joy of real fulfillment. To grow is to move toward the Infinite. We are constantly in motion and change. The only real constant in life is change.

If we don't grow, we must give in to the curse of mediocrity or permanent failure. Growth is to realize your purpose on earth. Without it there is the constant plague of meaninglessness. To find purpose opens the door to all virtues known to humanity. A knowledge of purpose is the foundation of patience. If you know the purpose of suffering, you can endure any degree of discomfort. If you have a "WHY" for living, you can survive the most difficult "HOW."

Forget the game playing technique when you are under pressure. The games people play are a mark of superficiality, and if you win, you have fool's gold for a prize.

MAKING DECISIONS UNDER PRESSURE

You can make the right decisions under pressure even if you have experienced failure in previous efforts.

The intensity of the pressure you feel is determined by your appraisal of the situation. Whenever you accept the responsibility of performing any task which makes demands beyond your resources you put yourself under pressure. Nobody can put you under pressure unless you permit it. You can reject the pressure at any given point if you decide to.

The first step in handling pressure is to relax. This is easier than it appears. Take a deep breath three times. Then count down from ten to one and with each count let go of another flexed muscle. This will clear your head for the next step.

Next, make a quick list of priorities. Don't feel pressured by the conflicts of life. What is the most important goal for you to accomplish right now? Maybe it is to maintain your health and not to win a battle. It's an empty victory to win a battle and lose your health. Dignity, too, is always more important than rules and regulations. Dignity takes priority over being right or intellectually accurate. Don't justify yourself to others. If they are your enemies no amount of justification will be enough, and if they are friends, you don't need any.

Forget the game playing technique when you are under pressure. The games people play are a mark of superficiality, and if you win, you have fool's gold for a prize. If you feel you are losing, you may over-play your game and become a fool. Nobody can make a fool of you; you do it all by yourself.

Resist the impulse to hurry. If you rush a person to respond fast enough, he will forget his own name. Try it on a friend, and watch him stammer trying to pronounce his own name. The Dutch have a saying, "The hurrier I get, the behinder I get." To hurry excessively can slow you down and reduce your efficiency.

When under pressure avoid stimulants. If you smoke, it is easy to be fooled by tobacco. Increased smoking gives the illusion of calming the nerves, but in reality it increases one's irritability, and the heart rate. When your energy is low the effects of coffee can deceive you. It over-stimulates the pancreas releasing insulin into the blood and it soon robs you of blood sugar and the energy you need.

Tranquilizers and alcohol are most dangerous in their deception when we are under stress. They may bring short term relief for anxiety and pain, but the habit forming consequences are destructive. Alcohol can cause the metabolism of sugar to be out of balance and this will increase the desire to drink. Long term abuse of alcohol is believed to form a new chemical in the brain that resembles morphine and this may explain the addictive nature of alcohol. Creating this unnatural state cannot benefit one when under pressure.

Proper diet and vitamins will help in making decisions under pressure. Long term pressure affects the immune system of the body. It destroys vitamins—especially vitamin C and the B vitamins. Doctors do not agree on the possible benefits of vitamins, so check it out for yourself. If you feel better, be thankful that you have found help.

Accept and love yourself. This will do more for you than anything else when you feel pressure. Give yourself credit for the skills you have developed. You should love yourself because your Creator loves you, and "He don't make junk." Human beings make junk from beautiful resources. That process can be reversed with your creative ability. Don't let negative imaginings distress you.

You can move into a situation which shows little promise and find some good in it to develop. This knowledge will help you in the noisy confusion of life to keep peace with your soul, and to make decisions under pressure.

*God grant me the serenity to accept
the things I cannot change,
The courage to change the things I can,
and the wisdom to know the difference.*

—St. Francis

THE DEATH OF A RELATIONSHIP

Separation anxiety bites deeply into the emotional life of anyone who has made great changes. It makes no difference whether you wanted the change, or if it were forced upon you. It still hurts, and remember: your motive for relationships will make a great difference in the way you feel.

There is no way to measure the awesome power and intensity of the pain one feels at the traumatic time of the loss of a loved one. Experts who study suicide claim that suicide as a result of a loss of love ranks with heart disease and cancer as cause of death. Suicide prevention centers report that 80% of their cases involve a loss of love. Some people feel that life has no meaning for them if a relationship is lost. Food is tasteless, self-identity becomes a problem, and often all perception of a future disappears.

When we experience loss or significant change, we go through the psychological stages of bereavement. At first we don't *believe* it is happening. We then get *angry*, and ask "Why me?" *Fear and uncertainty* is followed with an attempt to *make an equitable deal* with reality, so we can handle it. Then comes the *peace of accepting* what cannot be changed.

This last point of acceptance is not easy. It is difficult to escape the first four stages. Also, we may be tempted to use them to gain attention, sympathy, or to escape dealing with life's tasks. If we desire, we can stay there and be upset all of our lives, or—by choice—we can move on to a mature attitude and accept what cannot be changed.

Divorce hurts, even if wanted. The feeling of separation is devastating. The change that takes place touches the soul on many levels.

Without children a divorce is less complicated, but still has inherent problems. No one to *share* our joys or hurts. No one to see our accomplishments. No one to encourage us in failure. Sharing is a basic need for most of us, and we are particular with whom we share. If a man could mount to Heaven and view this great universe, his appreciation of its beauty and splendor would be not fully realized unless he had someone to share in his pleasure.

In divorce, life's interests are often diminished. Values become significant in relation to others. If the *other* is gone, the value seems to be less apparent. Self-condemnation will inevitably surface. "Did I do the right thing?" "Should I have waited?" "Should I have done something else?" "Did I make every effort to be sure?" These questions may be after the fact, but they still pursue the divorced. In divorce everyone will ask, "Is there something wrong with *me*, that my marriage failed?" If marriage fails, it does not imply failure as a person. One's marriage can fail simply because one has grown more rapidly than the mate.

The presence of children often complicates the lives of the divorced. Children respond emotionally to conflict. A divorce may provide a better life and less conflict than some marriages. Even so, it is traumatic for a child to deal with divided loyalties.

Divorce is a dark night experience because of the quiet,

subtle feelings that seem to ridicule our integrity and self-worth. Remember, these feelings are only false hints, and not reality-based emotions. The feelings are real, but they are not a measure of self-worth. Don't allow your search for answers to lead you into a false conviction of guilt when there is no real basis for it.

The intensity of the reaction to the loss of a relationship is directly related to the length or intensity of relationship. Reference points of personal identity are often related to our relationships. When they disappear we feel lost and often begin to ask "Who am I?"

At this point you must define yourself. Describe what makes you tick. Remember you are an important part of the universe.

> *You are a child of the Universe,*
> *No less than the trees and the stars;*
> *You have a right to be here.*
> *And whether or not it is clear to you,*
> *No doubt the universe is unfolding as it should!*
>
> —Desiderata

Fear is not a thing in itself. It is nothing but a shadow cast by other emotions.

DON'T BE AFRAID OF FEAR

Don't be afraid of fear—you create it. Fear is not a thing in itself. It is nothing but a shadow cast by other emotions—emotions that we create to deal with our sense of lack. Fears are imaginative creations used by the individual to alleviate a sense of boredom. We sometimes create problems and fears just to make life more interesting.

Most fears are symbolic. One will fear dirt when he feels unclean. One may fear the dark when he feels life is uncertain; another may fear the opposite sex because he feels that he can't cope with such relationships. When occupied with these fears the mind then is set free from dealing with real issues. The fact that these fears may be symbolic does not mean that they are groundless. Our reason demands that there be some justification for our fears; so we choose fears that are half truths. For instance, if you fear germs, there is some remote possibility that you might touch a door knob following a diseased hand (if it were still warm, contact the germs, etc.), but only a remote possibility. But there is enough truth that the mind can accept some degree of logic in it; otherwise it would be much easier to reject.

We need not be afraid of fear because we create it ourselves. Ambition casts a shadow of fear. When we create phoney goals to appear very successful we are trapped by ambition. We become fearful that we will not reach our goals. Our boasting brings fear. Our fear is in direct ratio to our desire to "get."

Pride is a game we play to express our hostility and create the illusion of personal superiority over others. Pride casts its shadow of fear. Without recognition our pride is hurt; so we fear what others may say about us. Pride prevents fulfillment. We can't be ourselves with this fear.

The perfectionist is such by choice, but we then live by fear. We can't move freely. We can't live spontaneously for fear that we will make a mistake or appear to be imperfect. We protect ourselves with a barrier of rituals and rules. We are so legalistic that happiness is impossible for us and those around us. We can't live and let live. Because of our fear we place distance between ourselves and others by constant fault finding. We can't contribute much to life because that is not our goal.

Greed creates fear. The feeling of greed is endless. It cannot be satisfied. Gain only stimulates the desire for more.

Even the fear of death is a shadow cast by ignorance. Those who live creatively and lovingly lose their fear of death. Death to them becomes another form of life.

We create ideas, dogmas, and prejudice in lieu of living unselfish lives of service and creativity.

We create our own fears for an excuse to live selfish lives. We need not fear anything which we create ourselves.

Unfounded fears are basically side shows in life's big event. These fears lead one away from the activity in the main tent.

HOW TO FACE YOUR FEARS

"Face to face" with fear is an encounter that demands honesty and integrity. Like all emotions, fear has a purpose. It awakens you to take precautions against harm or loss. The purpose of fear is to make you aware of the dangers that exist in any risk and to prepare you to meet them. We must admit that fear could be a manifestation of wisdom as well as a game to avoid life. Either way, we must admit that it exists and deal with it directly in order to rechannel it to our advantage.

This encounter should not be attempted without previous fortification. Our first step in dealing with fear is to seek knowledge. The unknown sound creates an eerie feeling of ghostly presence. An unknown cause for any event darkens the picture and creates an atmosphere of intrigue. When we search until we know the cause we often end up laughing at our fear.

Secondly, we must use our self-esteem to enable us to pursue life's problems and conquer fear. Self-esteem is an equitable estimate of our ability to face life and solve its problems. When we see ourselves as having resources beyond the confusion of the moment, we can be reassured that we can handle the outcome. At this point fear is replaced by an awareness of confidence.

A realistic appraisal of hostility will allay our fears. Hostility is an opinion of people, not an attitude of the universe. Neither God nor the laws of nature are hostile. Our fear of nature: (storms, flood, temperature) disappears when we realize that we are not the target. An electrical storm is a movement and release of energy and electrical charges. If we are in its way, we can be hurt. Nature does not intend to destroy us. The universe is a friendly place. We need not fear it.

One way to cope with fear is to ask questions:

> *What is the worst that could happen?*
> *Is it likely to happen?*
> *What will it really cost me?*
> *What am I afraid of losing?*
> *How do I know it will be bad?*
> *What can I do to limit my loss?*

The most powerful of all forces which can allay fear is love. What can love do about fears? When we experience love we become less concerned with the possibilities of danger, hurt or destruction. The experience of love fills this consciousness to the exclusion of superficial things. When we experience love we have a tendency to be more realistic. We tend to discard the superficial. So the experience of love acts as an expulsive power to push out thoughts of less important things. "Perfect love casts out fear" (I. John 4:18).

Love is a positive factor in life's experience; therefore, it will neutralize the negative factors of fear and doubt. Unfounded fears are basically side shows in life's big event. These fears lead one away from the activity in the main tent. The main tent, or the big show, is reality, fulfillment, responsibility, love and creativity. When we feel that we are not successful in the main tent, we don't want to deal with the events in the main tent, and thus the side shows become an escape.

We have a tendency to live on the periphery of life when we are not sure where the center of the target lies. Start searching for the focal point of the center of the target; start searching for the main event of life. Search for creativity, fulfillment, a meaningful existence, and it will be amazing how quickly the incidental, unimportant concerns and fears fall away. Fear will lose its grip on you. Meaninglessness is always swallowed up by a meaningful existence. Fear is always cancelled out by confidence. Love destroys hate as a light dispels darkness. The positive neutralizes the negative. Optimism erases pessimism. The big question is, "How do I do it?"

First change your focus from the negative to the positive. Focus on the good in your life, even if you think it's rather small; as you focus on it, it will grow. Secondly, visualize the success you wish to achieve. See yourself doing the things that are related to that successful venture. If it's money you want, see yourself spending it, handling it. Your fear of poverty will disappear. If it's love that you want, visualize yourself looking into the eyes of your beloved. If it's a new home you wish, see yourself walking through the door, relaxing and enjoying the beautiful home that is now yours.

Face your fears head on, armed with the strength which love gives. You will find fear quite impotent. Project yourself into the future and into the situation which you desire most. As sure as there is a God in Heaven you will move toward your focal point. Just as the boy, in Hawthorne's, *The Great Stone Face*, came to resemble the face because he gazed upon it every day of his life.

Focus on love.   Cancel fear.   Find peace.

Make more out of your life than a continual defensive operation against pain. If you protect yourself from feeling pain you also prevent yourself from feeling pleasure.

TRUSTING OTHER PEOPLE AGAIN

There is simply no way to grow and make progress without taking chances. No meaningful relationship can be formed without trust. Since we grow faster through meaningful relationships, it is to our advantage to trust others.

The question is one of timing and selectivity. Don't push yourself into a relationship too quickly. Wait until you feel the inner urge for more than you can offer yourself alone. Hurried relationships often end as abruptly as they began. Let your self-esteem grow until you feel you can trust without losing your inner peace.

Once you have been deceived you acquire inaccurate generalizations, false beliefs, and destructive habits. You may feel it necessary to be cold to the opposite sex. You may believe that everyone is a liar. You may develop the destructive habit of projecting that belief on to everyone. If you cling rigidly to a false belief, you will impede your own growth. Until you yield to the truth you can never succeed as yourself.

You can set yourself up to be deceived and betrayed. Our subconscious mind works like a computer. We feed into it hundreds of impulses when we meet a potential partner. We know what is likely to happen if we get close. We are better judges of human potential than we want to admit. If we expect to get hurt, and believe it, we will program it into the relationship.

When a friendship goes sour we sometimes ask, "What is wrong with me, that this could happen?" If you hang on to this inferiority feeling, it can prevent your trusting others because you feel so unworthy. This may be a defense mechanism used to avoid the risk of rejection. If you openly criticize others, they may reject you. If you criticize yourself you can escape the risk without rejection. They may even baby you.

Make more out of your life than a continual defensive operation against pain. You are supposed to feel both pain and pleasure. If you protect yourself from feeling pain you also prevent yourself from feeling pleasure.

Defenses take the threatening feelings and fears and set them aside. They distort your view of the world to meet your expectations. If you remain rigid, you will never be free to make new judgments. You will not reevaluate. You will not grow. Ultimately you will no longer be able to protect yourself in a changing world.

When you are realistic you grow. Remember, other people grow too. Give them the same chance you want in life. You will experience failures and successes, and so will others. You will experience joy and pleasure if you will only be open to them. Have the courage to accept your imperfections. You are human. Allow others the same privilege.

*If you take chances, you grow,
If you grow, you become your best,
If you become your best,
    you find happiness.
Relax, you won't be hurt as much
    as you may think.*

There is no power on earth as awesome as the power of the human mind. Many lives have been transformed by the power of choice. A decision to change which is executed by the mind has power that staggers the imagination.

WHAT CONSTITUTES A DRUG PROBLEM?

Many business firms display the following sign:

> "Difficult jobs we do easily, the impossible takes a little longer."

Those who never attempt the impossible still believe that it is impossible. What we believe—will be. Habits are not changed so easily as glibly saying, "O.K., let's change it." One who tackles the impossible with conviction that it *will be* cannot be defeated even when it is a habit involving one's own body.

Is it possible to throw crutches away when no longer needed? Many do so after using them for years, and some in the instant of time when they believe they can walk without them. Call it healing, autosuggestion, or whatever, the important point is that there comes a time when they no longer *need* crutches to walk. They are *convinced*—they *believe*. A crutch is good if used when needed, but a horrible liability when used unnecessarily. To use a crutch when you have two good legs only limits your ability to function. So it is with drugs.

Anything which chemically changes your mood is a fooler. Some users say, "I feel more alive and creative." There is never *more* of anything under the influence of chemicals. If one desensitizes four of his five senses dramatically, he imagines the one left is more acute only because he is less aware of the other four. Even the one left is less than it could be at its fullest potential. One can never realize one's fullest creative potential when desensitized by the use of chemicals.

Drugs become a problem, and not an aid to health, when they are not needed in order to function. A chemical high is an attempt to experience orgasmic fulfillment with the inevitable loss of the goal pursued. It is a flight from reality which produces a distorted vision of life. Addictions are exaggerated habits which we inflate to hide the shallowness of our inner life, and our lack of self-sufficiency. We use addiction to ward off loneliness. It reveals a weakness in self-esteem, and is a distress signal that we cannot find our way.

The answer to the drug problem can be found in the experience of a spiritual and intellectual high. In meditation one can release oneself from pain, stress, fear, and loss. The mind controls the body so completely that you can reach any goal desired.

Our real problem is to dismiss the conscious mind with its doubts, fears, and negative suggestions, and let the subconscious take over and produce positive benefits.

There is no power on earth as awesome as the power of the human mind. Many lives have been transformed by the power of choice. A *decision* to change which is executed by the mind has power that staggers the imagination. If your desire to change your use of tobacco, alcohol, or drugs is strong enough for you to make a *decision*, nothing, including your own physical habits, can stop you from carrying it out to fulfillment.

Mountain climbers reach the top only when they decide

to take one more step, even when totally exhausted. It is the determination to carry out a decision to get there that brings success. No one has been cured of drug abuse without making the decision to be free from its curse. It's not easy to be so determined, but it is possible for everyone who has any power of choice at all. If your power of choice seems to apply only in little things, exercise it daily to expand its effectiveness. With every successful choice you develop the power to make a bigger one. When exhausted, *take one more step*, and you will reach the top of the mountain.

In your darkest hours, when you suffer defeat, remember, the last chapter has not yet been written.

WHEN HOPE IS GONE

The feeling of hopelessness has invaded nearly every human heart. It is the most devastating frailty humanity is heir to. At times it seems that there is no alternative to our trapped condition. Every avenue appears blocked and every door appears shut. On our deserted sea of life the port of safety is out of sight, and we feel that possibly it doesn't even exist.

What do you do now? First, be thankful for the resistance you feel. Walking on ice is treacherous. Pure ice gives no resistance, no progress, and creates a fear of falling. There is a more secure, sure-footed feeling when your foot meets dry land.

Also, when life crowds you with problems and the weight of the world presses upon you, time is on your side. Like sand in an hour glass, it all crowds up at once, but passes one grain at a time. No matter what life presents to you, hours and days can only come to you one moment at a time. Let your problems pass before you one at a time and the burden will become lighter.

Cry, don't be afraid of tears. They are your floodgate to a

release of pressure. When your problems are significant enough to express feeling and shed tears, you create a two direction waterway. Your burdens will flow from you, and some of your most significant blessings will flow to you on your tears. Tears will clear the vision and you can better see the real values of life through tear-washed eyes.

Remember—burdens are necessary if you are to have a meaningful existence. We tell little children the tale of the old man and the clock. The old man looked with pity upon the old clock which stood in the hall for a hundred years. He said, "You've carried those heavy weights so long. I'm going to give you a rest." So, he lifted the weights off, and the clock stopped. "Please", said the old clock, "I can't run or be useful without my burdens. I can't tell time, nor ring out the hours. Please, give me back my weights." The old man returned the weights and the clock was happy once again. So it will be with you. Without obligations and duties you will feel useless. Without burdens you will lose the chimes in your life.

There is a solution to every problem, and it is not as far away as you may think. Many a person has lost life in a blizzard just yards from home because they stopped and gave up. One of the most impressive speeches Winston Churchill ever gave to a college audience was only one minute long, and contained only a few words. He was asked to give the students advice on victory. He stood to his feet and with all of his forcefulness said: "*If you want victory, never, never, never, quit.*"

Refuse to give up. God has planned His best for you. If you have missed the path by some great mistake, or even an injustice of life, keep moving. Sail on as Columbus did. Sooner than you think you will discover a whole new world of fulfillment and a meaningful existence. When Hillary climbed Mt. Everest he referred to it as his most trying hour of exhaustion. Someone asked him what he did in that hour and he said: "I took one more step; it is the only way to climb a mountain."

Keep moving, and when you get to the top your mountain will not be as impossible as it may seem. In your darkest hours, when you suffer defeat, remember, *The last chapter has not yet been written.* By sheer exercise of your will you can write that last chapter someday just the way you want it.

V

EMOTIONAL SELF-RELIANCE

To choose the right emotion for each occasion without being influenced by habit is an expression of self-reliance.

EMOTIONAL SELF-RELIANCE

To direct the thrust of our emotions is a mark of maturity. Ability to control our emotions does not mean that we are absent of feeling.

To choose the right emotion for each occasion without being influenced by habit is an expression of self-reliance. If custom decides for us, we are never free. Maybe all of our friends would react in the same manner to a given situation. Does that make it right for us? No—their emotions may be beneath our dignity.

Strong feelings often push dignity out the window. Some will say, "I just can't help what I do when I'm angry." Nonsense! We do whatever pleases our sense of values. If revenge is sweet to us, we'll get it. If it is not, we will let it go.

Emotional self-reliance is a commitment to value and dignity above the call for expression. *It is not necessary to do something about everything that happens.* Some words are best left unsaid. Silence will often be heard above angry voices.

Nothing is ever logical in emotional response. You can be free of bondage and independent to react the way that suits you. Don't be fooled by one who says, "It is only logical to fight back—hit him." If it is valuable to you, do it. If not, reject it. Remember that your emotional reactions will carry over into the days to follow. Do you want the results which your response will bring? Will it pay off in costly embarrassment or sorrow? Will you be proud of your reputation?

Emotional self-reliance means that you can stand on your reputation, and acknowledge your behavior. You can look with satisfaction upon your chosen emotional response, and say, "I'm glad I did it." When the dust settles, and each event is history, what do you have then? Your solitary hours will reveal your own self-approval or self-rejection. Your goal is to know the difference before you react. Self-reliance is the knowledge that you will make the right choice—the choice which will harmonize with your afterthoughts without regret.

Having emotional self-reliance is to be independent, and yet desire relationships. It is the ability to respect yourself, and yet let others feel that they too, have their place.

Self-reliance is a judgment which you place on your own opinion. It is not colored by prejudice, nor is it determined by custom. It is freedom from fear and guilt because you have done your best. Your best is all you have, so live up to it. It is your only way to grow. As you grow toward maturity you will reach new horizons of insight and knowledge, and each new vision will bring its own reward. Accept it—it's your future.

To deal with hurt, one must be realistic. People with unrealistic expectations never seem to be satisfied. After a while they expect to be let down.

HOW TO DEAL WITH HURT

Being hurt is experienced by every active, creative person. Life has its disappointments for everyone, but they can't dominate the soul who refuses to let them.

To deal with hurt, one must be realistic. People with unrealistic expectations never seem to be satisfied. After a while they expect to be let down, and soon find themselves wallowing in self-pity. A realistic approach to life acknowledges that we are all both good and bad, and yet, we all have value. We can emphasize our failures or our positive characteristics. It depends on our mood which we choose.

When you are hurting ask yourself, "Is it possible for me to grow by this experience?" It isn't easy, but it can be done. It will be easier than you may think. This is dealing with your feelings directly. This is necessary or your world will always seem to be getting out of control. Remember—some fears, some pain, some anger must be dealt with if one is to grow and be free.

Activity, the more consuming the better, is an antidote for hurt. To sit and lick your wounds will only cause you to magnify them. Activity will demand your attention elsewhere and soon your hurt can be forgotten for the privilege of living and experiencing newness. Physical exercise, a new task, a sport, or a mental diversion can be a life saver.

Find somebody who needs your help. Give yourself to a task that will be profitable to someone who can't repay you. Your hurts will sometimes shrink when you compare them to the helpless around you.

When you are hurting count your blessings. What do you have that you would not give up? What do you enjoy that you don't want changed? Is there anyone with whom you would actually trade places? To every one you find, you will find a million with whom you would not trade.

Forgive yourself. You don't have to hurt until you no longer feel guilty. Others may want to control you with guilt, but you can easily break that bondage. Forgive yourself for your failures.

Make a commitment to change, and be sure that the changes are for your good. We change for the best by seeking a higher level of honesty in feeling, and by learning to accept ourselves and others as we are. We can be blind to our faults or our needs. Without honesty there will be no change. Instead of change we will repeat our negative experiences just to prove to the world and ourselves that we are right.

Promise yourself a new life—a better life. Your plan, your vision, your commitment will bring it about.

It is strange that two words that sound so much alike should point in opposite directions. It is only when we pause to look at our motive for relationships that we see the difference.

LONELINESS ???
ALONENESS ???

    We are solitary, unique individuals, whose deepest fears and hopes may never really be *fully* shared with another person. We each have our own private logic and individual philosophy. The manner in which we express our uniqueness will determine our aloneness or our loneliness.
    Aloneness is a beautiful experience of freedom and oneness with creation. Life has meaning for you on many levels.
    Loneliness is the experience of fear and darkness. One feels lost, and incapable of finding direction. It is an awesome awareness of being empty.
    What you accumulate determines your sense of loneliness. When you fear the thought of losing, on any level, you feel lonely. Some think the accumulation of material possessions will bring security and happiness. They feel that money will solve life's problems. We accumulate emotional reactions to protect us from loss. For example, we get angry when insulted, and this protects our loss of pride. We accumulate beliefs to protect us from pain; such as, the pain of death is lessened if we believe we shall meet again. We accumulate intellectual patterns to protect us from failure, so we feel at

ease when we can do things as we have always done them. We are frightened of the unknown, but feel comfortable with the familiar. When we let go of these accumulations we become one with the universe and therein find peace. Letting go is an attitude. To let go of the unnecessary is to be alone.

Aloneness is enjoyed by mature people who do not feel that they must be entertained. It is the basis of our greatest strength and in aloneness great works of art, song, and literature are created.

Loneliness is our greatest weakness. It is the emptiness felt by a leaning, dependent individual when he or she has no one on whom to lean for comfort and support. They want to be entertained so they will not be aware of their fear of facing the world alone. They are likely to remain lonely because their dependent attitude keeps them nonproductive and shallow, and others find them boring.

Aloneness is the independent inner life of those who have let go of possessiveness. They have let go of the desire to compete. They have let go of the desire to dominate, and to exploit others. In aloneness we let go of all the unnecessary accumulations.

Aloneness is a fullness of spirit and knows no feeling of poverty.

It is strange that two words that sound so much alike should point in opposite directions. It is only when we pause to look at our motive for relationships that we see the difference.

Introversion or extroversion is a mental habit rather than a description of behavior.

INTROVERT ???
EXTROVERT ???

Introvert—Extrovert—those words are commonly used to describe behavior. She is talkative, sociable, outgoing—she is an extrovert. He is shy, quiet, withdrawn—he is an introvert. These concepts are true, but much, much more is implied in the words. There is a significant spiritual depth to these characteristics. They actually describe one's search for meaning.

Introversion or extroversion is a mental habit rather than a description of behavior. Introversion is the tendency toward being predominantly concerned with self. It is a narrow interest in one's own mental life. Extroversion is the habit of directing attention toward the world. It is a tendency to find gratification from what is outside the self.

If you are an introvert, it need not spell social failure. Many factors can cause the introvert to shut out the world and withdraw. When one is confused he stops, looks for answers and finding none, withdraws into a "safer" inner world. One then begins to look within for answers to life's conflicts. This going within can contribute to one's maturity and sense of responsibility. Here you may find the answer—if it is your problem. You will not find the answer within to all of your social success problems because the answer may lie within the value system of the other person. You can't blame yourself for another's basic mistaken assumptions about life. Basic assumptions about life form a foundation for each person's private way of looking at each situation. This becomes his private logic. Every move in life is based on this private logic.

As an introvert, one may look within so much that they have no opportunity to express themselves socially. On the other hand, extroverts look to others for approval and are in danger of losing their own value system in an attempt to become socially successful. Extroversion can result in seeking an ever evasive reward, and, as in *Dante's Inferno*, leave one continuously groping because social success is impossible without a stable value system.

On the surface it is easier to get acquainted with the extrovert, but this doesn't mean that the extrovert actually has more friends than the introvert. You may be either and have social success.

Where is the middle of the road? To some it is a negative fear. It is halfway between telling everybody to "go to hell" and the fear that everybody will tell you to "go to hell." It is actually a comfortable, happy place where one is sure that one is free to be oneself and is not intimidated by one's environment nor the people in it. Don't be intimidated—you have a right to express yourself.

You must be independent—yet care how others feel, but don't care *too much*.

You must be loving—yet demand respect.

You must give—but save some for yourself.

You must be able to receive—without feeling obligated or indebted.

To be happy, you must protect your own sense of being free to be yourself.

You must let go of old habits if you are to become intimate with the existing moment. Live now! Let each moment be a lifetime of freedom to think, to plan, to experience, to create.

HOW TO SURVIVE ONE DAY AT A TIME

The father of individual Psychology, Alfred Adler, used to say: "If you had to have a rule for swallowing, you would choke to death." Exaggerated self-awareness, and a competitive approach to life narrows our whole view of life and the world. Conformity to patterns breeds stupidity and a superficial contact with life. It causes us to worry about the future by demanding servitude to authority and society. It makes relaxation impossible. We want rules to live by, and the rules choke us.

To live one day at a time is the path to enlightenment. It is good "horse sense." A horse will graze from one clump of grass to another. In a day's time he will move hundreds of yards without any thought of how he got there. He moves from one spot to another. He enjoys every minute of the process without analyzing his movements and without constantly reestablishing his goal. His moment to moment fulfillment has been its own reward.

We have so exaggerated the importance of our planning power that we often become slaves to it. The conscious, planning intellect is powerless to free itself from the conditioning of the past. We like to shuttle back and forth within the limits of old habits and old formulas.

If we live exclusively by the intellect, we fail to use our inner light, and miss the adventure and joy of being creative. To act on impulse becomes a crime, and we limit ourselves to the beaten path. We sit down to eat without thought of analyzing our next move. If we were to eat our meals and take each bite by rules and formulas, a feast would lose all attractiveness.

You must let go of old habits if you are to become intimate with the existing moment. Live now! Let discovery guide you to a new awareness of living. Take some time to do as you please. Let each moment be a lifetime of freedom to think, to plan, to experience, to create.

There is nothing that can happen today that you and God together can't handle. Remember that tomorrow can't be experienced until it gets here. Its problems may disappear before they actually arrive, like the diminishing ripples of a pebble dropped into the water. Its power diminishes with every wave. Jesus said, "Can you add one moment to your life by worry?" Let go of tomorrow. It will be different than you think; so don't waste time that could be used to make today more meaningful.

You have today. Live every second of it to the fullest, don't waste your energy on worry. Save your strength. When tomorrow comes you will have strength for the task at hand.

Life by the inch is a cinch,
Life by the yard, is hard.

Even prisoners of war who were biologically depressed by malnutrition have conquered that depression by singleness of purpose.

UNDERSTANDING DEPRESSION

Depression is a silent temper tantrum displaying one's displeasure with life's events. It is a double-bind which produces various stages of inertia.

The human mind is unable to pursue two targets simultaneously. Conflicting goals make forward progress impossible. Depression is always based on conflicting goals.

It is basic to provide for selfish needs. When these selfish needs conflict with our desire to appear righteous, we find ourselves at an impasse. We feel like a dog chasing two rabbits, and catching neither. When the rabbits go in opposite directions it is impossible to chase both. If we refuse to give up either, we lose both.

This impasse is experienced on many levels. Dividing a candy bar illustrates my point. If I were to owe a depressive person fifty percent of a candy bar, and I break it fifty-fifty, there is no problem. We can both take half and all is well. If the bar is broken sixty-forty, there is conflict of goals. It is now impossible for the depressive to take the big piece and appear to be an unrighteous pig. It is impossible to take the small piece and cheat the personal need to be selfish. With both choices impossible they are stopped short, and angry because they have no candy. Either choice is good and both choices are bad; so they cannot take either. Now they are at an impasse and angry because they have lost control of the situation. Depression results.

Depression is composed of three basic factors: A need to control, a need to be righteous, and a need to express selfishness. When these needs are in conflict depression appears to be the only choice. When control is lost the depressive worries further into depression.

When depression is based on hypoglycemia or some other biological pathology, medication can be helpful.

If depression is based on psychological factors, it will never be resolved with medication. It is necessary to come to terms with conflicting goals. Goals must be evaluated in light of the payoff offered by each. All human behavior has a payoff inherent within. When the payoff is unreal the goal must be discarded. If a goal costs too much to be realized it must be discarded. When the cost, in values, exceeds the results, in experience, a goal is worthless.

Life is too short to be wasted on meaningless investments. Make your choices based on what you sincerely believe to be right and let the chips fall where they may. Then move on to life's next chapter. There is more to learn, more to see, and more to experience. Don't miss it.

Most situations, about which we are angry, are rather insignificant when we analyze them. We plague ourselves with anger even when it profits us nothing.

WHAT DO I DO WITH ANGER?

Nobody can make you angry. It is a matter of choice. Anger can be dismissed at will, or indulged to your detriment. Dismissing anger is much easier said than done. Anger is a reaction to a situation which displeases. Your reaction to any situation or event is a matter of *choice*. When displeased or violated one may react by attacking or withdrawing, with tears or laughter, with silence or screams.

Your value system will be the basis for your choice of reaction. If you want to rid yourself of anger, look at your values. You are displeased with your anger because of conflicting values or conflicting goals.

Anger is an *emotion*, it is not a *reason* for action. It is only the steam we generate to drive us toward our goal. When one says, "I did it because I was angry", that is not facing reality. We should say, "I chose to get angry in order to act faster", or "I chose to get angry in order to avoid the responsibility for my actions." The nature and direction of our actions is determined, not by our emotions, but by our basic value system.

When one uses one's likes and dislikes as a compass to

find which way the emotional wind is blowing, it is sure to pile up on the rocks of reality. Our likes and dislikes are a thermometer which measures our maturity under the heat of pressure.

Most of us protect our likes and dislikes as if they were precious jewels. If they are threatened, we whip up a storm of anger to scare off the intruder. If we examine the threat carefully, we find that nothing much is threatened except our prejudice. Most threats are insignificant. Most emotions would die on the vine if not watered by our tears.

Analysis dissipates emotion. If anger plagues your life, and seems to be ever present, pick it apart. Ask yourself several questions. Why am I angry? Is it important? How valuable is it? Does it have meaning? Will I feel the same tomorrow, next week, next month, next year? How will it affect my life in years to come?

Most situations, about which we are angry, are rather insignificant when we analyze them. We plague ourselves with anger even when it profits us nothing.

Anger increases the flow of adrenalin, changes the heart beat, increases blood pressure, overworks the delicate balance that keeps us healthy. Anger expressed accomplishes so little and when not expressed, damages so much.

Redirect your anger. Project yourself toward a meaningful, creative goal and use the energy generated by anger in a constructive manner, and donate your anger to a good cause. This will rechannel your energies from destructiveness and remove the obstruction to your peace of mind.

Jealousy is an endless, lonely journey. It is an angry method of asking for reassurance and never getting it.

HOW DO I COPE WITH JEALOUSY?

Jealousy is the green-eyed monster that devours the delicate heart of any interpersonal relationship. It destroys happiness, and under its cruel vice-like grip the joy of companionship is squeezed out of existence. It is an obnoxious symptom of a more serious condition of the inner self. It is much more than just a refusal to share one's love partner. It is the expression of an inner dependent relationship in which one fears loss of a treasured possession. In an attempt to hold on, one actually alienates the other person, and creates distance. In an attempt to protect one's territorial imperatives, the jealous person attacks the beloved rather than the suspected intruder. It is possible to proceed to attack the suspected intruder without proof of guilt. The result is that the beloved becomes a prized possession and thus, a non-person. The jealous rage alienates and destroys. In jealousy, we find that we not only lose the one we would possess, but we also lose our personal dignity and self-respect. Any relationship based on jealousy lacks dignity for all involved.

Is there redemption for the jealous heart? Yes, but it is necessary to go beyond the symptom and deal with the cause. Jealousy is an expression of insecurity, lack of self-esteem, an impoverished sense of self-worth, and a fear that we can be replaced. This fear and insecurity can cause us to come to the conclusion that we are unable to deal with life's problems and solve them. There is a fear that relationships will be destroyed, and in an attempt to preserve the relationship we destroy it ourselves by finding fault, making thrusts of blame and accusations which are received as personal attacks.

There is a subtle psychological twist here. Without realizing it, the jealous persons would rather destroy the relationship because of what they "do" rather than because of what they "are". One of humanity's most significant problems is to distinguish between "doing" and "being". What we "do" can be changed at a whim. What we "are" is basic to our existence. To change what we "are" is a lifetime process. It is almost unbearable to lose a relationship because of who we are. If it is lost because of what we "do", it is easy to conclude "It was just my foolish acts, and not my personal worth that caused the loss." We can change our behavior even if we feel trapped with what we are. The partner of a jealous person will ultimately conclude that all relationships will be evaluated negatively. For example, coming home from a party or social gathering the partner will ask, "What did I do wrong now?" After repeated accusations the accused will only want to escape the relationship permanently.

The true expression of personal feelings is the only solution. To express fear and insecurity honestly is not an attack upon your partner, and will not have the alienating effect of criticizing the other's behavior as the cause of your uneasiness.

Jealousy is an angry method of asking for reassurance and never getting it. If you want reassurance, change your focal point from criticism of the behavior of others to talking about your inner feelings of frustration and discomfort. Never *blame* the other person for your feelings if you want the relationship to grow.

Jealousy is an empty void which can never be filled. The more you feel it, the more it will absorb. To explain and defend behavior to a jealous person is like casting pebbles into the sea. One could take lie detector tests, provide witnesses, and prove innocence but the jealousy will not be abated because the true cause is being ignored.

Jealousy is an endless, lonely journey. Remember, your feelings are always a matter of choice. They may be logical, consistent, and even seem to be appropriate, *and* they are always chosen. The behavior of others is never a cause of your emotions. You interpret the behavior before you come to a conclusion of how you feel about it and react.

The mastery of any emotion is in your power of choice. You have absolute control of feelings. Thank God for this power, and use it wisely.

Your weight is under your control. Master it, and the sense of well-being to follow will be worth the effort.

WEIGHT CONTROL AND YOUR EGO

The most significant factor in weight control is your mental attitude. You will never lose weight until you make a decision. Most people plunge into a diet on impulse. Many are angry and going to show the whole damn world that they can lose weight; or they may be angry with themselves for looking so out of shape. When you're motivated by anger to change your weight, the diet usually runs its course just about as rapidly as your anger. In a few days you'll be over your anger, and in a few days you'll be over your diet.

Some people lose weight because of their wardrobe; it's cheaper to lose weight than buy new clothes. That is a good reason to lose weight, but obviously it is not a strong motivating force because it didn't motivate you to keep your weight down in the first place.

Some people lose weight because they want to be attractive to a stranger of the opposite sex. The diet usually holds up until the stranger is no longer a stranger, and then the diet fades as does the newness of the relationship. Most relationships do not help us stay thin.

Visit your doctor, make sure there is no glandular malfunction or biological cause for your gaining weight. If there is, then treat the biological problem before you attempt to lose weight or accept the challenge of a diet.

It's time to be serious about your weight when it is difficult to bend over and tie your shoes. When it takes more effort to climb in and out of an automobile, it's time to think about shedding pounds. When your breath is short from climbing one flight of stairs it's time to take action. Remember, every pound of excess weight that you carry puts added strain on your heart, and shortens your life.

Some want to lose weight for the cosmetic effect. This is a good reason, but it soon loses its force and drive. Most people conclude that it just isn't worth the effort.

It's easy to manufacture a compensation to deal with excess weight. Some attempt to laugh it off; we see them as the fat, jolly, happy people enjoying life. This is one attempt to deal with excess weight—laugh it off, but it doesn't laugh off the weight. Another form of compensation is the aggressive heavy—they come on heavy, they attack, they criticize, they push, they "throw their weight around", and we soon find them unpleasant, and avoid them because their weight is too heavy for us to carry psychologically.

Excess weight can be a very good barrier—it's easy to build a wall of fat around yourself to keep the world out, but remember, it also keeps you locked in. Many obese people feel rather secure in having a reason for not getting close to anybody. It enables them to avoid intimacy: "It's my excess weight that keeps me from being popular, or from having a good time socially."

Another good reason for being overweight is to escape life's tasks. You will never be asked to do some things because people know that with your weight you just can't do it; so you have a logical excuse.

Whatever your reason for being overweight, you must

decide its true value. Is it worth the price to be overweight? Is it worth the price in shortened years, and the inability to move around?

There is a way out of your prison of fat, if you want to escape. After you have seen your doctor and received confirmation that there is no physical abnormality causing your problem, move on to a clear-cut psychological plan that will enable you to lose weight and keep it off.

The first step in your psychological strategy is commitment. Make a commitment to yourself that you will reach a certain weight by a specific date. Be gentle with yourself, don't rush into the strategy of losing weight. It's absolutely impossible for you to lose a hundred pounds in two or three weeks, and maintain reasonable health. Many of the crash diets do nothing more than take water out of the system, and the scales appear to be lighter, but the fat is still there. Remember that your commitment is a promise to yourself, and promises are kept by sheer willpower. Some say, "I just can't help myself, I have to eat." Yes, we have to eat, but we don't have to eat many of the foods that we devour. When you make a commitment to yourself to lose weight repeat it daily. Soon you will program your eating habits to harmonize with your commitment. Every morning remind yourself several times, "I have made a commitment to lose weight. Today I am going to carry out that commitment, today I will do whatever is necessary to meet the demands of that commitment." Later in the day when you sit down at the table, remember your commitment; and when the pie and ice cream come your way, you'll be satisfied with two bites, rather than two pieces. Tell yourself that two bites of a delicious pie is just two bites better than none—and much more satisfying than to feel stuffed when you know you shouldn't have eaten it. Repeat your commitment each time you sit down at the table—repeat your commitment before and after each meal—soon you will find yourself quite selective about the foods that you eat.

Keep a diary. At the end of each day write down the foods you ate that you did not need. Also, make a list of the foods that you could have eaten but passed by, and thirdly, make a list of the foods that you really wanted but avoided. In making your diary, you will soon learn that there are some foods that are absolutely not fattening at all. There are some foods that you can "stuff on", and never gain weight. You don't have to leave the table hungry.

Another psychological strategy that will help you in losing weight is to buy some new clothing. Don't buy the size you wear now, buy the size that you want to wear six months or a year from now. Hang it up in your bedroom where you can see it every morning and every night. Look at the new clothing and promise yourself that on a certain day "I am going to be able to wear those new clothes." This is an extension of your commitment, your commitment to your own future.

Your weight is under your control. Master it, and the sense of well-being to follow will be worth the effort.

VI

MAKING THE MOST OF MATURITY

THE BRIDGE-BUILDER

An old man, going on a lone highway,
Came at the evening, cold and gray,
To a chasm, vast and deep and wide.
The old man crossed in the twilight dim;
The sullen stream had no fear for him;
But he turned when safe on the other side
And built a bridge to span the tide.

"Old man," said a fellow pilgrim near,
"You are wasting your strength with building
　　　here;
Your journey will end with the ending day
You never again will pass this way.
You've crossed the chasm deep and wide,
Why build you this bridge at eventide?"

The builder lifted his old gray head
"Good Friend, in the path I have come," he said,
"There followeth after me today
A youth whose feet must pass this way;
This chasm that has been as naught to me
To that fair haired youth may a pitfall be;
He, too, must cross in the twilight dim—
Good Friend, I am building this bridge for him."

　　　　　　　　　　—Author Unknown

DOES AGE MAKE A DIFFERENCE?

As in the mellowing of wine, age can make you better. As a better person, life can be more meaningful and enjoyable. Mark Twain's vision of heaven, in which he was privileged to choose his age for eternity, expresses man's desire for maturity. At first he elected to be a ten year old boy, and soon found that he desired to be a young man. Each stage lacked something. As he finally moved up to his mature age of eighty, he said, "This is my choice for eternity."

Mature years will not bring perfection, nor should you permit the experience of past failures to blind you to the fulfillment ahead. You are not perfect and sometimes your mistakes may block you from your goals, but there are countless goals to pursue. When you make a mistake give yourself understanding. Under difficult conditions you have an opportunity to show your true worth. Build your self-image by rethinking your successes instead of your failures. Failures are inevitable, but they are only events. They cannot make you a failure as a person. Thomas Edison, after thousands of failures in his invention of the light bulb, referred to them as a learning process. In his successful completion of a light bulb that worked he said that he had found thousands of ways that it could not be done. Look upon your past failures as a learning process, and you will be better prepared to execute the successes of tomorrow because you have learned how not to do many things.

Many successes come only in mature years. Grandma Moses, in all of her fame, did not start painting until her 75th year. Col. Sanders became famous for his national success with fried chicken after the age of sixty-five. Dr. Albert Schweitzer, famed at 95 as the greatest physician of the century, did not start medical school until age forty-three. Sir William Mulock, on his ninety-fifth birthday, spoke to his friends who were honoring him on this occasion:

> *I am still at work, with my hand to the plow, and my face to the future. The shadows of evening lengthen about me, but morning is in my heart.*

Keeping his "hand to the plow" at ninety-five is the secret that kept him young.

History gives proof that mental powers increase with age, that artistic and intellectual powers are intensified in later years. Michelangelo was still producing masterpieces at age eighty-nine. Goethe completed *Faust* at age eighty-two. Wagner finished *Parsifal* at age sixty-nine. Handel was composing music after seventy. Some of the greatest tasks ever accomplished were undertaken after the so-called retirement years.

Age does make a difference. You have greater capacity for growth as you get older. Under the age of fifty most people do not know what they want. It takes many years to learn what really brings you happiness.

Self-expression is most significant in later years because

you *have more to express*. Sometimes a childhood dream is picked up after retirement and amplified into a whole new life. It may then be better executed than when you were younger.

Wear your gray hair proudly like a flag. You are fortunate that in a world of conflict and change you have lived long enough to earn it.

Use your skills and you can maintain them with ease. Disuse starts the ecological process into action. Everything not in use must go back to the earth.

USE IT OR LOSE IT

What do you enjoy most in life? List six things that you really like to do. How often do you do your favorite thing? Most of us will have to say, not as often as we would like. We lose the opportunity to do what we want because we do not pursue it earnestly. The small tasks of life so fill our time that the momentous experiences are overlooked, and soon we realize that they are no longer a part of our lives.

That feeling of well-being that comes from vigorous exercise is lost because we are too busy. First the feeling of well-being is lost, and then the muscle tone and strength is lost because we don't use it. A good exercise program helps us keep our youth longer than any other physical factor.

Youth is maintained by attitude. General MacArthur was asked on his eightieth birthday, "How does it feel to get old?" His reply surprised them when he said, "I don't know, old age is an attitude." He kept youthful vigor through his mature years because of his attitude. An elderly real estate saleslady was asked why she still worked full time and was a leading salesperson. Her answer revealed her secret, "I just refuse to get hardening of the attitudes." If your attitude is young, you will be youthful. Use your positive attitude, or you will soon lose it.

Use your skills and you can maintain them with ease. Any artistic ability becomes rusty with disuse. Simple hand movements would be lost if we were to totally stop using our hands. Disuse starts the ecological process into action. Everything not in use must go back to the earth. Even an unused nail will rust and disappear.

Your physical strength and sexual vigor will remain as long as it is put to use. Your body is like a computer constantly making read-outs and adjustments. If a reserve of strength is stored too long without use, the cellular structure of the body changes to release the unnecessary reserve. If it is called upon for use, it replenishes the reserve. If not, it is released to enable the body to adapt to the type of life of your choice. There is no need for sexual vigor that is never called upon, and your body will adjust accordingly. You must use it or lose it.

Every emotion is an experience which we have chosen. We set ourselves up for the feeling we decide is appropriate for the occasion. As long as we can use any given emotion it lingers on. If a negative emotion produces desired results, you can use it for a life time if you so decide. If you desire to get rid of it, stop using it and it will subside. The same is true of positive feelings. If you stop using them, you will lose them. We may not want the responsibility for our feelings, but it is a glorious privilege to be able to control them and decide our destiny. This power of choice is "image of God" within us. Believe it, and it is yours. Refuse to use it and you lose it!

To be seventy years young is sometimes far more cheerful and hopeful than to be forty years old.

—Oliver Wendell Holmes

SEX AFTER SIXTY

Sexual pleasure diminshes after sixty *only for those who believe it does.* There are significant changes in the body as one grows older, but they are not necessarily destructive changes. The sexual experience can grow richer, and more meaningful.

The mature male has a better sense of timing than he had in his earlier years. He now has the ability to control his sexual impulses and he can prolong the sex act to greater satisfaction. In his earlier years it was all over in seconds. The duration was disappointing in his youth, both to him and his partner.

The mature female is more relaxed in the sexual relationship. The fear of childbirth is nothing but a memory. The concern for child care is a thing of the past. A new freedom is available to her if she wants to claim it.

Maturity fosters a spirit of unselfishness. In earlier years sexual fulfillment was sought in selfish satisfaction. Now personal fulfillment is found in the partner's satisfaction. This brings a more beautiful type of experience which is more rewarding for both parties.

In earlier years the sexual experience was like diving into a pool with a big splash, and climbing right out again. In mature years it is moving into a warm pool in slow motion permitting the warmth to penetrate throughout the whole person. This makes it possible for sexuality to go beyond the physical and become a part of the soul. Body, mind, and spirit should be blessed by sex, and not just the genitals. When rushed, the rest of the body doesn't have time to get in on the act. This may explain why younger women often prefer older men.

In mature years one can make sex a big deal because the problems of material world are usually put into second place by then. Personal experience becomes more important than material accumulation.

As we grow we become more like the Oriental who looks upon sex as an event with significance. The Oriental custom is to let the sexual experience reach into hours of bathing, eating, caressing, knowing, and finally copulation.

The physical body need not stop functioning when we reach the eighties and nineties. Good diet, regular exercise, proper rest obey the physical laws regulating use of the body functions. Good habits aimed at good health will enable you to be active sexually all of your life.

Don't be fooled by fables and myths that sex is lost with age. With maturity it only becomes better.

Your attitude will produce in reality what you visualize. What you see to be important will color every word and deed in your life.

WHAT YOU SEE IS WHAT YOU GET

Young or old, life has much to offer. If you view life from the right perspective you will see what it has to offer. The right perspective is to see life through positive emotions of serenity, lightheartedness, and hope.

Laughter is the best avenue by which to develop a good perspective. Norman Cousins, long-time editor of the *Saturday Review*, is the most celebrated case of recovery from a supposedly irreversible disease. In the famous account of his recovery, it is indicated that laughter, faith, Vitamin C, and a positive mental attitude reversed his illness and started him on the road to new health. Ten minutes of genuine belly laughter had an anesthetic effect, and would give at least two hours of pain-free sleep. Laughter is good medicine. There is healing power in the mind which can be activated by laughter. Laughter stimulates positive emotions. Positive emotions produce positive chemical changes, just as sure as negative emotions produce negative chemical effects. Develop a good sense of humor. Learn to laugh and you will see life in a new way for the first time.

Pretend you are going to open your eyes tomorrow

morning for the first time—you have been blind all your life. What will you see for the first time? Instead of just trees you will see ten thousand leaves on one tree. You will see beauty in the lowly weeds at your feet. Every color will be special and almost personal. Life has so much more to offer than most people see. You will begin to express your thankfulness for the privilege of being alive. You will be thankful for the little things which make life possible. A thankful heart will help you to see *life* for the first time.

Accept responsibility for your life and the way it is going. You will see life differently. You will see the potential for changes that is available to you. If you have chosen your life strategy, then you also have the power to change it. Your life is in nobody's hands but yours. Your future can be as different as you want it to be. If you had only six months left to enjoy life, what would you change? You would stop worrying over the next ten year's problems. You would forget the opinions of friends and neighbors. You would enjoy the value of little things as well as big things. You would pack 60 minutes of living into every hour. You would see *life today* for the first time.

Your attitude will produce in reality what you visualize. What you see to be important will color every word and deed in your life. If your attitude has been negative, you have limited your blessings. You have rejected life because you couldn't see it.

An attitude of hope and positive feelings will produce a new picture of life for you, and *what you see is what you get.*

You are sure to go beyond the obvious. You will see your own reflection in your work, and you will find answers BEYOND THE ROPE'S END.

THE CONFLICTS OF AGING

In later years it is easy to lament lost opportunities. As you look back you ask yourself, "Why?" Why didn't I buy gold when it was thirty dollars an ounce? Why didn't I move to the great frontier of Alaska? Why didn't I go to school longer?

These conflicts of thought can be disconcerting if you dwell on them constantly. Remember when you were half your age you only had half a picture before you. Your decision then was based on the information at your disposal. You are making decisions now based on the view you have. If you live another lifetime, you will see today as having limitations of perspective. Don't condemn yourself for limitations which are not yours.

Conflicts can arise over a desire to do more physically than your strength will allow. If you have this conflict now, you probably had it years ago. We keep our attitudes toward physical strength. If a young man can lift two hundred pounds, he has inner conflict because he wants to lift three hundred. You haven't changed that much, so just relax and enjoy the strength you have and it will stay with you as long as you use it.

Another conflict of age is your discouragement with the contemporary scene. If you look back, you will remember that your parents were confused about your ideals and your expressions of life which differed from theirs. Our constant search for truth and knowledge will produce changes in each generation. Whether we want to admit it or not, the trend of civilization itself is ever upward. We have more discoveries to control disease and prolong life than ever before.

The future looks bright. We are marching along an endless pathway of unrealized possibilities of human growth. When you feel that you have reached the end of your rope remember you have made a greater contribution than you think. If you are not satisfied with your life, it is never too late to start over. You are a part of a new world. Opportunities for individual achievement were never greater. We stand at the gateway of tremendous new developments.

You are a part of a divine cosmic destiny which you may never fully understand. Project yourself into the future by doing all that you can on every level. You are sure to go beyond the obvious. You will see your own reflection in your work, and you will find answers BEYOND THE ROPE'S END.

Notes

Notes

Notes

Notes

Notes

Notes

Notes

Notes